Coastal Walks around
Anglesey

Porth Wen near Bull Bay (walk 9)

Coastal Walks around
Anglesey

*Twenty two circular walks exploring the
Isle of Anglesey Area of Outstanding Natural
Beauty*

Carl Rogers

MARA BOOKS

First published in May 1996 by **Mara Books**,
22 Crosland Terrace, Helsby, Cheshire WA6 9LY.
Telephone: 01928 723744

Reprinted 1997, 1999.

Second edition May 2004.

Third edition August 2008.

ISBN 978-1-902512-20-4

All enquiries regarding sales, telephone: (01928) 723744

Acknowledgements

Thanks to Bob Nash, Jack Rogers and Audrey Rogers for checking all
the walks.

British Library Cataloguing-in-publication data.

A catalogue is available for this book from the British Library.

Contents

Introduction

A NGLESEY lies off the coast of North Wales separated from the mainland by the Menai Strait—a flooded valley less than 300 yards wide at Menai Bridge and a little under a mile wide at Caernarfon. Geologically the island is an extension of the coastal plain which stretches north and west from the mountains of Snowdonia, but its character is very different. The Pre-Cambrian rocks of its foundation are very old—some of the oldest in the world—with overlays of younger shale, visible at Parys Mountain, and limestone, which can be seen in the east of the island around Penmon and Llanddona. On top of this there is a thick covering of boulder clay and glacial drift, giving the island its rich fertile soil.

The occasional visitor en-route to the ferry terminal at Holyhead, whose only view of the island is the 20 miles of undulating farmland seen from the A55, could be forgiven for

*The southern end of the Menai Strait with the hills of the
Lleyn Peninsula in the distance*

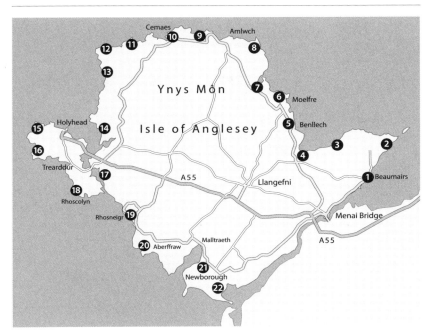

feeling rather indifferent to this sometimes mundane landscape. In poor weather the monotony of the interior can be almost oppressive. The reason is its underlying structure—a series of flat, low-lying valleys running across the island from northeast to southwest. In fact Anglesey contains one of the few really large areas of flat land in North Wales. There are few points within its 290 square miles that rise above 400 feet, but where this does happen, such as at Mynydd Bodafon (walk 7) and Holyhead Mountain (walk 15), the views are extensive and the feeling of height exaggerated.

Thankfully, unlike the interior, the coast is anything but dull and unchanging—in fact Anglesey can boast some of the finest and most varied coastal scenery in Britain. The uniform plan of the island—looking a little like the letter 'Q' tipped on its side—has not resulted in a lack of detailed interest around the coast. There are wide tidal estuaries, sandy bays separated by rocky headlands and dramatic cliff scenery sheltering quiet coves.

Climatically, the island has much to recommend it, being one of the driest and mildest parts of North Wales. Often, you will be able to enjoy hours of warm sunshine here, while the highland areas of Snowdonia just a few miles away lie draped in mist and rain.

This close proximity to the mountains gives the island another big advantage over coastal areas elsewhere. Except on parts of the north coast, the mountains provide an ever-present backdrop to intricate coastal foregrounds. This interplay of coast and mountain produce such unrivalled views as that of the Lleyn Peninsula and its shapely hills from the beach at Aberffraw (walk 20) and Ynys Llanddwyn (walk 21) and Newborough Warren (walk 21).

Footpaths and access

For those exploring on foot, there is excellent access to the island's ever changing coastline and for much of its length there is a well maintained coastal path. This is constantly being improved under the management of the Isle of Anglesey Coastal Path Team, with the aim of providing a continuous path around the entire island (www.angleseycoastalpath.com).

This is complemented inland by a vast network of public rights of way which are also being improved with new stiles and waymarkers. Should you encounter any problems, either on the coastal path or public rights of way away from the coast, please refer them to the *Rights of Way Unit, Highways, Transportation and Property Department, Council Offices, Llangefni LL77 7TW. Telephone: (01248) 752 300.*

A brief history of Anglesey

A NGLESEY has a rich historic heritage with visible remains of settlement reaching back into the second millennium BC. In fact the island has one of the highest concentrations of prehistoric sites in Britain.

The position of Anglesey, thrust out into the Irish Sea, along with its gentle terrain and the rich fertile soil of the interior, have ensured that it has been populated from the earliest times. In

Bronze Age standing stones at Penrhos Feilw

the 1,500 years before the Romans conquered Britain, various tribes settled in these islands and their method of travel, both for exploration and trade, seems to have been primarily by sea. As such, Anglesey was ideally placed at a crucial point in the seaways of western Britain. Unfortunately, this has also made it vulnerable to attack and invasion, which became a major feature of its early history.

The fact that Anglesey was densely populated in prehistoric times is made evident by large numbers of megalithic tombs, which provide the earliest visible remains of settlement on the island. Fine examples can be seen in the fields near Traeth Lligwy (walk 6) and Rhosneigr (walk 19). Visitors to the restored burial chamber known as Bryn Celli Ddu near Llanddaniel Fab, can see the original form of these monuments.

The next phase of settlement—known as the Bronze Age— brought immigrants who have come to be known as the 'Beaker folk' (from their distinctive pottery) to Anglesey towards the end of the second millennium BC. It was these tribes who raised the island's many standing stones, although their purpose remains a mystery.

By the fifth century BC, Celtic tribes had begun to move into Britain and by the time of the Roman conquest, Anglesey is thought to have been one of the most important centres for the Celtic or 'old religion' in Britain. The writings of Julius Caesar suggest that the Druid religion was developed in Britain and exported to other Celtic tribes in Northern Europe. If this is true Anglesey would have been one of the most important religious centres in Europe

This religion was taught by a class of priests known as 'Druids' and it seems to have been they who stirred up the greatest resistance to the Roman occupation of Britain. There seems little doubt that it was to stamp out this seat of spiritual resistance, that the Roman leader Suetonius Paulinus set out to invade Anglesey in AD 61. With an army of over 10,000 he crossed the Menai Strait and in one easily won battle extinguished the old

Celtic religion completely. The sacred groves were destroyed and the Druid priesthood wiped out.

The fact that so little is now known about the Druids and indeed about much of the early history of the Celts, is due to the fact that they committed nothing to writing; all their religious teaching and history was passed on orally. All manner of fanciful and gruesome practices have been attributed to the Druids but nothing is really known about them for sure. Their knowledge and traditions died with them on the shores of the Menai Strait almost 2,000 years ago.

British settlement at Din Lligwy

It was the Celts who introduced the Iron Age culture to Britain and their most enduring legacy is the many hill forts which can be seen all over the country. Anglesey is no exception and a number are visible today, with fine examples at Holyhead Mountain (walk 15) and Bwrdd Arthur (walk 3). Perhaps the most impressive remains from this period are to be found at Din Lligwy (walk 6) near Moelfre. Here the visitor needs little imagination to visualise the settlement as it was—hut bases, doorways and enclosure walls are all clearly visible.

Despite its length—over 300 years—the Roman occupation left surprisingly few remains on Anglesey, which was probably controlled from the fort across the Menai Strait at Caernarfon (Segontium). The most notable remains are to be found at Holyhead, where the walls of a coastal fort still enclose the church and the base of a lookout tower—known as Caer y Tŵr—stands inside the old hill fort on Holyhead Mountain.

If you stand on this summit today, you will enjoy a fine view out to sea in all directions, but on a clear evening out to the west you will see the Wicklow Mountains of southern Ireland, and it was from here, when the protective arm of Rome had been removed, that raiders came in the early post-Roman era. These invasions inevitably resulted in settlement and it may be significant that the hut circles on Holyhead Mountain are known today as 'Cytiau'r Gwyddelod' or the 'Irishmen's Huts'.

The Irish invasion became such a problem that a powerful Celtic chieftain or Romanised Celt from Strathclyde, came to North Wales with a large army commanded by his sons and devoted the rest of his life to ridding the land of these invaders. His name was Cunedda and it was in a last battle on Anglesey that the Irish were finally defeated and expelled from Wales in about AD 470.

Cunedda established himself at Aberffraw where he built a palace close to the site of the present day village (walk 20). In doing so, he founded a dynasty which would rule North Wales for almost eight centuries and produce such notable

Misty isle—a view across the unusual lowlying interior of Anglesey to the mountains of Snowdonia

leaders as Rhodri Mawr, Gruffydd ap Cynan, Owain Gwynedd, Llywelyn Fawr (the Great) and his grandson Llywelyn the Last, whose defeat by Edward I in 1282 brought a final end to Welsh independence.

The reign of Maelgwyn Gwynedd, a descendant of Cunedda's, saw the firm establishment of Christianity in Anglesey during the sixth century, with the founding of monasteries at Penmon (walk 2) and Holyhead by Saint Seiriol and Saint Cybi. Although he is said to have been a wicked ruler, the land on which these monasteries were built was granted by Maelgwyn. Perhaps he was looking for divine favour towards the end of his 'sinful' life.

The rule of the Welsh princes is unfortunately a rather sad period, being marked more by treachery than any great

The church at Penmon stands beside the ruins of the priory

advancement. The progress made by some of its greatest rulers was often destroyed by the infighting of their descendants. This was caused in part by the tradition of dividing a man's possessions equally between his sons following his death. The result was that at best his kingdom was much weakened, particularly if he had many sons, which was often the case. Siblings thus became rivals and frequently fought each other for their rightful share of their father's lands. Rivals were often eliminated or imprisoned. Prince Llywelyn for example, is said to have held one of his brothers in Castell Dolbadarn near Llanberis for over twenty years. Others made alliances with former enemies outside Wales in a desperate bid to gain their birthright.

This lack of unity—a trait first noted by the Romans—was quickly exploited by Saxons and Normans keen to expand their lands and influence. It also meant that when threatened, Wales as a nation was never able to defend itself with a united force.

During the early years of the ninth century a new menace presented itself; one that came to be feared throughout the British Isles and one that Anglesey was particularly vulnerable to—Viking raids. By this time the Vikings had formed colonies at Dublin and in the Isle of Man and from there they launched attacks all along the Welsh coast. The monasteries at Holyhead and Penmon were attacked in 961 and 971 and the palace at Aberffraw was partially destroyed in 968. The Vikings left no settlements on Anglesey but a number of names remain as evidence of their passing; notably Priestholm (Puffin Island) and The Skerries off the northwestern tip of Anglesey.

The Norman conquest had little impact on Anglesey initially, although an early raid by the Earl of Chester in 1090 led to the building of a motte and bailey castle at Aberlleiniog (walks 1&2) near Beaumaris. This was soon destroyed by the powerful Gruffydd ap Cynan and the Normans made little real progress against the Welsh for the next 100 years.

When the threat of Viking raids ceased towards the end of the

15

eleventh century, a period of prosperity followed and with an increase in population, a programme of church building began. It was at this time that churches were first built in stone and a number have survived, in part, from this period, notably Hen Chapel near Din Lligwy (walk 6).

It was also during this time that deforestation of the interior of the island was finally achieved, releasing rich fertile land for agriculture and earning Anglesey the name 'Môn, Mam Cymru'— *Anglesey, Mother of Wales*. This referred to the vast quantities of grain which were grown here during the Middle Ages, sufficient it is said, to feed the whole of Wales.

During the wars of Llywelyn Fawr and his grandson Llywelyn the Last, the importance of Anglesey's ability to feed Wales was realised and both King John and Edward I made attempts to take Anglesey, thus depriving Wales of its food supply. It was the loss

The coffin of Princess Joan at Beaumaris

Beaumaris Castle

of Anglesey which finally brought Llywelyn Fawr out of hiding in the highlands of Snowdonia to bargain with King John and ensured Edward's victory against Llywelyn the Last in 1282.

Following his conquest of Wales, Edward I embarked on a programme of castle building all along the North Wales coast, the ruins of which still stand. On Anglesey he built his last Welsh castle at Beaumaris in 1295 near the site of one of Llywelyn's courts at Llanfaes.

Wales was now subject to the English crown and the title 'Prince of Wales' reserved for the king's eldest son. The wars of independence were over, although Owain Glyndŵr was to raise the Welsh banner briefly at the beginning of the fifteenth century.

The Skerries lighthouse

Although Wales was never to see independence from the English crown again, it did produce one of the most influential ruling families ever to sit on the throne of England—the Tudors. The seat of this family was Plas Penmynydd in Anglesey and Henry Tudor's claim to the throne came through his descent from Owain Tudor and his rather mysterious marriage to Henry V's widow, Queen Catherine, in 1429.

The late sixteenth century saw an increased demand for copper, required for the production of cannons and a host of household items. The Tudors were instrumental in restricting the import of foreign metal and the subsequent rise in the price of copper created great demand towards the end of the seventeenth century. The abandoned mines at Parys Mountain and the development of Amlwch as a port, are the result of the discovery and exploitation of one of the richest deposits of copper in the country.

The heyday of the industry was between 1760 and 1815 and the higher wages offered by mining took many workers off the land during these years. Another industry from this period which we can still see remains of today, is that of milling. A number of old windmill towers remain as testimony to Anglesey's former corn production.

Anglesey's position adjacent to the Liverpool sea lane and its proximity to Ireland have produced a rich maritime history. By the seventeenth century, packet boats were regularly crossing to Ireland, providing a service which was to expand in the nineteenth century when Thomas Telford completed his London to Holyhead coach road (A5) and built the graceful suspension bridge over the Menai Strait in 1826.

Anglesey's rocky, treacherous coastline presented a constant hazard to shipping and there were literally hundreds of shipwrecks during the nineteenth century alone. The most famous wreck was that of the *'Royal Charter'*, which hit rocks and sank off Moelfre in 1859 with the loss of over 400 lives. The lighthouses which dot the coast today date mainly from this period although they are now all automated.

Today, tourism plays a key role in the island's economy and with road improvements on the mainland cutting the travelling time from Merseyside and Greater Manchester, Anglesey has become a popular venue for weekend breaks and second holidays. Away from the coast however, agriculture still dominates, although the emphasis is now on cattle and dairy farming, with little or no sign of its once famous corn fields.

Beaumaris

Distance: *5½ miles*

A gentle easy walk centered on the historic town of Beaumaris. The coastal section is along the shore and subject to suitable tides, with a return by field paths and quiet lanes.

Start: There are numerous places where cars can be parked in Beaumaris, along with two large long stay car parks. Begin the walk outside the castle entrance opposite the 'White Lion Hotel'. A section of this walk is affected by the state of the tide. Consult tide tables before starting (see note below).
Grid ref: 608 760 (Landranger 114, Explorer 263)

The walk

1. With the castle entrance behind you turn left along the road passing a play area on your left. About 80 yards after traffic lights, bear right down a one-way road. Follow the short road to the waters' edge where it turns sharp right. Turn left through a kissing gate here and out into a field. Go ahead on the path which runs close to the crumbling cliff edge overlooking the Menai Strait.

This path gives fine views out over the Menai Strait to the mainland where the rounded slopes of the Carneddau rise behind the coastal towns of Llanfairfechan and Penmaenmawr. To the east the weathered limestone headlands of Penmon and the Great Orme reach out into the Irish Sea.

The path now drops to the road. Walk ahead along the road until it turns away from the shore at the end of the bay. Drop down right onto the beach and follow the shore for about 1 mile.

Caution: High tides cover much of this beach and reach right up to the crumbling cliffs near Lleiniog—the shore is accessible apart from 1 hour either side of high tide. You will need about 30-40 minutes to complete this section, if the tide is low or falling there should be no problem.

As you approach Lleiniog there are some interesting formations in the cliffs which clearly show the layering and composition of the glacial drift which covers much of the island.

2. At Lleiniog bear left by the river which flows across the beach and at the road turn left. There is a surfaced footpath shortly on the right which runs parallel to the lane. Follow this path until

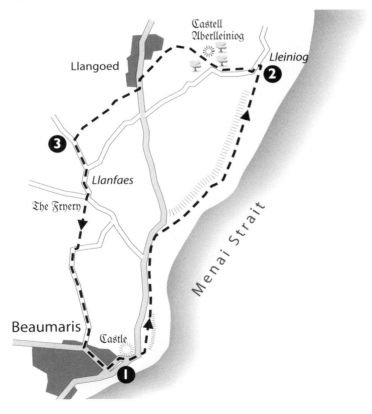

St Mary's Church, Beaumaris

it joins a path/track where the lane bends away to the left. Turn right here and follow the track beside the stream to join the concrete access road to the treatment works on you right.

The ruins visible in the trees to the right of the path are those of Castell Aberlleiniog, a Norman motte and bailey fort built by the Earl of Chester in 1090. The original structure was destroyed just three years later by Gruffydd ap Cynan causing the Normans to abandon Anglesey for the next 100 years. The present stone ruins are thought to date from the medieval period.

Walk up the road and turn left at the first house keeping to the left to join an enclosed footpath. At a T junction and kissing gate, keep left and walk beside gardens on the right eventually joining the road at Llangoed. Turn left here and after about 100 yards cross over and turn right onto a well used field path. After a stile enter a caravan and camping site. Walk through the site passing the toilet block and partway through an area of caravans, a yellow arrow on a post directs you half-right to a second arrow which indicates a right turn to a stile in the hedge behind one of the caravans. Walk half-left across two fields aiming for the Bulkeley Memorial high on the skyline.

3. Turn left into a narrow lane and continue to Llanfaes. The little church here is all that now recalls the site of Llanfaes, once the major trading centre of the island.

It was here that Llywelyn the Great had a court and founded the Franciscan Abbey which was to become the burial place of his wife Princess Joan, the daughter of King John, in 1239. Part of her stone coffin can be seen in the doorway of St Mary's Church in Beaumaris, but nothing remains of the abbey.

When Edward I decided on this location for his final Welsh castle, along with the adjoining borough of Beaumaris, the inhabitants of Llanfaes were evicted and moved to a 'new borough' in the exposed southwest tip of the island. Today this village is known as Newborough.

Where the lane bends sharp right, turn left (ignore first left to the church) and look for a small gate and fingerpost beside the

Beaumaris castle

large gate posts to 'The Friary'. Go through the gate and follow the right of way directly across the following field and golf course, rising to where stone steps lead into a quiet lane. Turn right here and follow the lane left around the bend and back to Beaumaris.

Beaumaris came into existence as a borough in 1296 with the building of Edward I's castle. The name is thought to be derived from the old French 'beau mareys' meaning the 'beautiful marsh'. The land on which the castle and the town stands originally lay on the edge of the Menai Strait and ships could dock alongside the castle walls. Much of the present town was thus built on reclaimed marsh land and its setting could certainly be described as beautiful—backed by the rich farmland of Anglesey with wide views across the Menai Strait to the mountains of Snowdonia.

Beaumaris was the last of Edward's Welsh castles to be built and although its construction covered a period of 30 years, it was never completed. It did however, see action in the Glyndŵr rising of the early fifteenth century and the Civil War in the 1640s.

The castle is unique in being the only one of the ring of fortresses with which Edward encircled North Wales to be built on flat low-lying ground. This enabled its architect, Master James of St George, to produce a symmetric design not possible at any other Welsh site. For this same reason the castle is sometimes disappointing to the visitor. It has none of the commanding skylines or dominating presence of Caernarfon, Harlech or Conwy. Its strength comes from its concentric defences. A moat fed by tidal water encircled the outer wall, which in turn presented a line of defence which, if breached left attackers little better off. The walls of the inner ward are even higher and the towers—positioned forward from the wall line—gave defenders a clear view along the outside of the walls.

The use of gunpowder in the late Middle Ages left castles defenceless and most, including Beaumaris, fell into ruins. Interest was only revived when visitors began to come to North Wales towards the end of the eighteenth century and during the Victorian period.

In 1925 Sir Richard Williams-Bulkeley gave the castle to the Commissioners of Works for preservation as an ancient monument. Renovation work followed and resulted in the clearing out and re-establishment of the moat on the west side and the removal of vast undergrowth which can be seen clothing the walls in many early drawings. Today the castle is one of the most popular attractions on the island.

Penmon

Distance: *6½ miles*

A varied route exploring the island's extreme eastern tip. The limestone walls, lush green fields and hedgerows are unusual for Anglesey and are confined to this sheltered corner of the island.

Start: There is a small car park in Llangoed. This is situated on the right, at the northern end of the village, just before the little bridge over Afon Lleiniog and the pub 'Tafarn y Rhyd'.
Grid ref. 611 797 (Ordnance Survey Explorer 263)

The walk

1. Turn right out of the car park, cross the little bridge and turn right again almost immediately onto an access road. Where this forks after a few yards bear right and follow the concrete road to a water treatment works on the left. Immediately before the works bear right onto a woodland path with Afon Lleiniog to your left and continue to a quiet lane.

Just before the lane you may just glimpse the ruins of Castell Aberlleiniog hidden amongst the trees on your left. This is the site of a Norman motte and bailey castle built by Hugh de Avranches, Earl of Chester in 1090. It stood on a mound which is still almost 30 feet high and over 150 feet wide and would originally have been built of timber. The present stone ruins date from the late medieval period.

This first advance into Anglesey by the Normans was short lived; the powerful Gruffydd ap Cynan captured and destroyed the castle just three years later. After this setback, Anglesey was abandoned by the Normans for over 100 years.

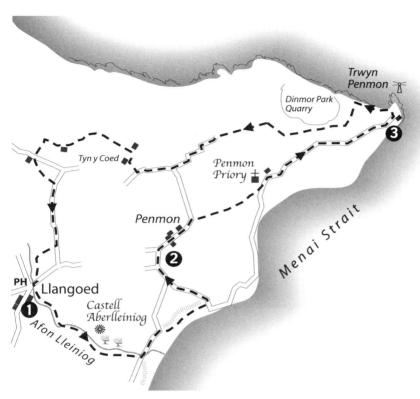

Immediately before the lane, turn left onto a surfaced footpath
and follow the path to its end where you will have to continue
along the lane. After the bridge over Afon Lleiniog pass a car park
on the right and continue along the lane to the signed coastal
path on the right immediately after a house ('Cerrig', also on the
right). The path leads between gardens and down steps onto the
shingle beach.

If the tide allows, turn left and walk along the shore to the
concrete embankment and road at the end of the small bay.
Turn left here and follow the lane to the first distinct left-hand
bend. (Alternatively, if the tide does not allow, reach this point
by continuing along the lane from Aberlleiniog). Bear right here
signed 'Penmon' (or turn left if you did not walk along the beach)

27

and at the next left-hand bend go straight ahead on a rising rough access road, then continue on a footpath between cottages.

2. At the top of the rise, turn right along the lane and walk through the tiny hamlet of Penmon

As the lane bears left beyond the houses, look for a signed footpath on the right which enters fields by means of stone steps and an iron gate in a high wall.

The right of way takes a direct line through a large field with the Great Orme directly ahead. Aim for Puffin Island at first, then as you approach a fence, bear right slightly then keep ahead again to begin a gradual descent. Lower down join a track which eventually passes a ruined church up to the left and leads to a large metal gate. Do not go through the gate (usually locked), instead, turn left and look for stone steps and a gate on the right just before the priory buildings. Go through the gate and turn left along the road.

The existing priory buildings date from the latter half of the twelfth century and housed a community of Augustinian monks until the Dissolution, when the lands were granted to the Bulkeley family. The site is traditionally associated with the monastery of Saint Seiriol, the sixth century friend of Saint Cybi who lived on Holy Island.

A popular story concerning these two friends relates how once a week they each walked half way across the island to meet at a well near Llanerchymedd. The walk to and from this central meeting place meant that Cybi had the sun in his face both morning and evening and became known as 'Cybi the Dark'; while Seiriol always had the sun at his back and became know as 'Seiriol the fair'.

Seiriol was a descendant of Cunedda, a powerful chieftain who expelled Irish invaders from Anglesey during the fifth century, and a second cousin of King Maelgwyn Gwynedd. The land on which he built his church at Penmon is said to have been granted by this royal cousin. Today, little or nothing from Seiriol's time has survived except the remains of his cell adjacent to the well.

The Celtic monastery that Seiriol established here suffered badly in the late tenth century when there were repeated attacks from Viking

Penmon lighthouse and Puffin Island

raiders all along this coast. Two carved stone crosses from this period can be seen inside the church.

After the Dissolution of the Monasteries in the sixteenth century, the land and buildings passed into the ownership of the Bulkeley family who established the deer park and built the dovecote about 1600. This impressive little building was built by Richard Bulkeley to house over 1,000 birds and would have provided an important source of fresh meat. Eggs would have been collected by means of a ladder supported on the central stone pillar which stands over twelve feet high.

Follow the toll road down to the end of the headland at Trwyn-du or Penmon Point (ignore a road on the left which leads to the quarry).

At the end of the road there is a small café and toilets which are open during the summer season. Just offshore, a tall black and white automatic lighthouse warns shipping of the dangerous sound between Anglesey's most easterly headland and Puffin Island.

This tiny island has at least three names, each telling us something of its history or character. In Welsh it is known as 'Ynys Seiriol', after Saint Seiriol who founded the monastic settlement at Penmon and built a second monastery on the island. In the following century Cadwallon, King of Gwynedd, was besieged here by Edwin, the Saxon king of Northumbria, during a time of Saxon expansion into Wales.

The ruins which can be seen today are the remains of a twelfth century church which replaced earlier buildings once the threat of Viking raids had ceased. This brings us to the island's second name: 'Priestholm' which is Norse in origin. The name refers to the monastic community which thrived when the Vikings first came here in the tenth century.

The only other building on the island is a small nineteenth century semaphore station, part of a chain which extended all along the coast from Holyhead to Liverpool. Messages were transmitted visually by means of signs supported on masts and movable arms. Though rather crude by modern standards, it proved to be amazingly effective in its day and could transmit a message from Holyhead to Liverpool in just a few minutes. The island's only inhabitants today are sea birds, among them puffins, from which it gets its most recent English name: 'Puffin Island'.

3. Walk back to the little café and bear half-right across the grass on the footpath which runs along the lows cliffs which back the shingle beach. At the end of the bay follow signs which direct you left (there are quarry workings ahead). At a T junction turn right onto a good path. Follow this path ignoring other paths to the right and left until a large ladder stile leads over the wall into grazing fields. Take a direct line through the first field, then turn right along the access road which leads into Dinmor Park Quarry. Immediately before the quarry entrance gate (about 35 yards), turn left through a kissing gate and walk through a large field keeping right beside the wall. In the field corner bear right through the gate or over a stone stile and keep beside the old deer park wall on your left.

Bear left over a stile at the head of the field and again stay beside the wall. In the corner of the field enter a narrow lane beside a small cottage on the right and walk along the lane for about 600 yards to the first junction. Go straight ahead here and after about 300 yards turn right down a drive signed for the coastal path. Immediately before the garden of the last house turn left through an iron kissing gate onto an enclosed footpath which shortly leads into fields. Keep to the left-hand field edge in three small fields and pass through a kissing gate beside a cottage. Turn left for a few yards and then right through a second gate adjacent to the cottage. Go ahead through the centre of a small field and look for an iron kissing gate in the far hedge (ignore a faint path down to the right).

Keep ahead in the following field to join an access track beside a small cottage. Follow the track and after a short rise, bear right following the signed footpath through an area of gorse. Just before a large gate leads into fields, turn left through an iron kissing gate and keep right along the edge of a large garden. At the end of the garden bear right through a second kissing gate and follow an enclosed footpath with a high wall to the right. At the end of the path turn right down a short drive to a lane.

Bear half-right here to where an iron kissing gate (coastal path sign) leads into fields again. Keep to the field edge and in the bottom left-hand corner of the field, stone steps lead over the wall onto a track. Turn left along the track keeping left at a fork.

At the end of the track a large gate and kissing gate lead into a quiet lane and a kissing gate opposite continues the right of way. Bear to the left through the centre of the field, following a faint track in the direction of the church to join the lane beside the cemetery. Turn right down the lane passing the school and look for a signed footpath on the right after about 600 yards. Keep to the field edge and at the bottom of the field, just before the corner, turn left passing a small cottage on the right. Walk down the drive to the road and turn right returning to point 1.

Llanddona

Distance: *5½ miles*

Undulating walking in an unfrequented section of the island with wide views across Red Wharf Bay. Footpaths are generally good particularly the sections used by the Isle of Anglesey Coastal Path .

Start: Drive into Llanddona from the south and bear right by the 'Owen Glyndŵr' public house. Just after the road turns sharp left on the edge of the village, turn right and park on the verge just before the lane forks.
Grid ref. 579 795 (Ordnance Survey Explorer 263).

The walk

1. Keep right at the fork (signed 'Eglwys Llaniestyn') and walk down the lane until the tarmac ends at a bungalow on the left ('Tyn Llan'). Turn left down the drive. Soon you will see Llaniestyn church behind the bungalow and as you approach the cemetery look for a stile in the corner to the right which leads into fields. Bear half-left in the first field aiming to the right of a small farm where a ladder stile leads over the wall. Walk half-left again through a smaller field aiming for an old iron kissing gate in the far hedge. In the third field keep to the right-hand field edge ahead and enter a narrow lane with 'Tyddyn Uchaf' farm to your right.

Turn right and walk along the lane for about ½ mile. Immediately before the first farmhouse on the left ('Cefn') turn left over a stile beside a large gate and follow a green lane which shortly leads into fields. Keep ahead along field edges.

At a large farmhouse bear right to a kissing gate. Turn left through the gate to join a track at the back of the house. Turn right and follow the track to the road.

2. Turn left along the road and take the first lane on the right signed 'Eglwys church'. Follow the lane passing the little church in fields over to the left and a little further on a house on the right ('Tŷ Mawr') where the coastal path joins from the right. Continue along the lane and where this swings right go through the gate ahead and follow the farm track to 'Tan Dinas'. Pass through the farmyard and follow the track ahead.

(To visit Bwrdd Arthur which is open access land, look for a faint footpath on the left which rises to the lane where a footpath climbs onto the summit. Return to this point to continue.)

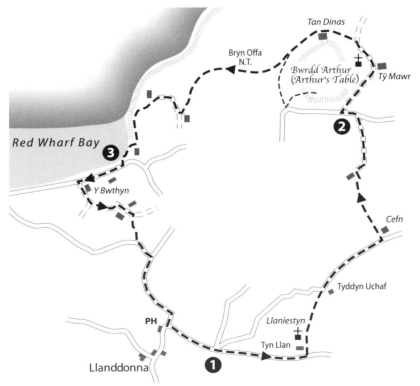

Bwrdd Arthur is an impressive limestone plateau and forms a natural fortress. It supported a British settlement similar to Din Lligwy near Moelfre (walk 6) during the Iron Age and early Roman period. Today, the remains, though far less impressive than Din Lligwy, can still be identified and include a defence wall (originally 5-8 feet thick) enclosing a site of almost 17 acres, along with the remains of several hut circles. Finds date mainly from the Roman period.

In clear weather you can enjoy uninterrupted views in all directions with features as far away as the Isle of Man, the fells of the Lake District and the Lancashire coast visible across the Irish Sea to the north.

Looking west across Red Wharf Bay from Bryn Offa

Eastwards, the limestone headland of the Great Orme stands beyond Puffin Island, with the lighthouse at Penmon marking Anglesey's easternmost point.

To the south, the high rounded tops of the Carneddau rise behind the towns of Penmaenmawr and Llanfairfechan, with the serrated outline of Snowdon further west. In the far distance, the triple peaks of Yr Eifl (The Rivals) form a backdrop to the cultivated landscape of eastern Anglesey. Westwards, the wooded slopes of Mynydd Llwydiarth fall to the wide sweep of Red Wharf Bay, with Benllech, Moelfre and Mynydd Bodafon beyond.

Continue along the farm track to a gate and ladder stile which lead into a large field. Turn right and keep to the field edge in the next two fields. In the right-hand corner of the second field, a stile leads onto National Trust land at 'Bryn Offa'. Descend through gorse and heather to join a track and turn left.

Follow the track to a fork by a cottage, turn right and keep right again at a second fork. Almost at the end of the track there is a small cottage ahead and a narrow field gate on the left immediately in front. Go through the gate and bear half-right across a small field to cross a ladder stile, then continue ahead to pass along the right-hand field edge overlooking the rocky shore. Continue to where a kissing gate and steps just before a cottage, lead down onto the beach.

3. Turn left along the beach to reach the road on the left by the coastal footpath sign. Turn right along the road.

After about 300 yards, turn left into an unsurfaced access road signed as a public footpath beside 'Y Bwthyn'. Pass the house and where the track swings right, continue ahead on the rising green lane. This climbs between high hedges to reach a house with wide views across the bay. Bear left, then right between the buildings following the rising access road. Shortly, within 100 yards or so, where the road bends left and immediately after a ruin on the right, take the signed footpath on the right. Go through the kissing gate and where the path forks almost immediately, bear left on a rising path through an area of gorse to eventually join a lane. Turn left up the lane.

At a T junction turn right and follow the lane back to the village of Llanddona.

Turn left by the 'Owen Glyndŵr' pub and return to point 1 to complete the walk.

There is little of note at Llanddona, although its secluded location and fine views of Snowdonia make it an attractive spot. It will also appeal to those who dislike Anglesey's flat interior; the walk up from Red Wharf Bay should have convinced you that this area is anything but flat!

During earlier centuries the village was known for its witches. Exactly who these were is unknown and each account gives a different explanation, although the descendants of shipwrecked Irish sailors are thought to have settled in this remote corner and, due to their unfamiliar appearance and language, were most likely feared by locals. This fear and suspicion could well have been encouraged in an attempt to conceal smuggling activities which were almost certainly carried on here. Anglesey is thought to have been an intermediate stage for contraband runners from the Isle of Man.

Red Wharf Bay

Distance: *4 or 5¼ miles*

A mixed undulating walk over tidal sands, marsh and through woodlands on an unfrequented section of the coast. Footpaths are generally good although care should be exercised with the tides (see note below).

Start: There is free car parking available on the shore at the southern end of Red Wharf Bay. This can be reached by taking the narrow lane ('Lôn y Traeth') which runs down to the bay from the B5109 at Pentraeth.

Caution—high tides cover much of the sand and marsh around the edges of the bay making walking difficult and even dangerous at certain times. Cars left on the beach may also be at risk from high tides. Consult tide tables and time the walk to coincide with a falling tide to be safe.

Grid ref. 535 798 (Landranger 114, Explorer 263).

The walk

1. Walk east (to the right when looking out to sea) along the edge of the sand and marsh for about 1¼ miles.

Just beyond a small wooden beach house a lane reaches down onto the sand. Here you have a choice. For a shorter walk turn right and walk up the lane for about ½ mile. Turn right into an access road and continue from point **2**.

For a longer walk, keep ahead on a signed footpath which soon follows the top of a sea wall.

After the sea wall continue ahead to a sandy track which reaches down onto the beach on the right (large aerial on hillside

Decaying hull on the beach near the start of the walk

above). Follow this rightwards to join a road which curves in from the left. Bear right along the lane for about 250 yards to a signed footpath and ladder stile on the right. Follow the path ahead to a gate and rise to a T junction with a more prominent track. Turn right here and contour the hillside to enter a small wood after the second field (stone farm building on left). Follow the path through the wood and enter a field by a metal kissing gate. Keep to the right-hand field edge and enter a second larger wood. Shortly the path forks—keep right here and remain on the prominent path for about 300 yards.

Although woodland clothed much of Anglesey until the early Middle Ages, trees are a rare sight in many parts of the island today, especially in the exposed north and west. Here on the east however, woods are more numerous giving the landscape a completely different look. The wooded hillsides which surround Red Wharf Bay make it one of the prettiest bays on the island.

The path emerges from the woods by houses; turn left up the access road. At the lane turn right.

2. After about 150 yards turn into an access road on the left (this will be on the right if you are coming up from the beach on the shorter walk). Walk up the access road passing houses on either side. After the last house the track enters the forest and shortly a junction is reached with a track on the left. Ignore this continuing straight ahead on the prominent forest road. Ignore a signed path and forest road on the right after about 400 yards and continue ahead for another ¾ mile.

At a large area of felled trees, stay on the prominent forest road ignoring a path which forks left into the clearing.

This clearing allows a fine view over Anglesey's interior set against a background of Snowdonia's highest peaks and the shapely hills of the Lleyn Peninsula.

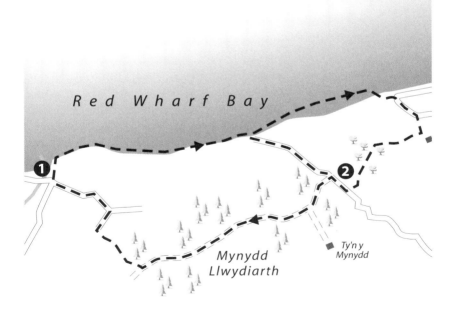

About 400 yards further on, a broad forest road joins from the left. Ignore this, instead, follow the track as it bears right and drops. At the bottom of the dip look for a yellow arrow on a low post directing you right onto a narrow but obvious footpath (the forest road begins to rise again beyond this). Follow the path through the trees and leave the woods by a stile. Ignore a crossing path and walk directly down the hillside through an area of rough heather and gorse with a wide view of the bay, to join an access track. Turn right down the track and at the first sharp bend go through a small gate straight ahead and turn right. Keep descending and at a T junction with a cottage to the left, turn left. Follow the tarmac road back to the car park to complete the walk.

Benllech

Distance: *4½ miles*

A short easy walk along an interesting section of rocky coast and quiet inland footpaths. The area is well walked with excellent footpaths.

Start: There are two large pay and display car parks in Benllech near the beach at the bottom of 'Bay View Road'. Begin the walk at car park entrance or the 'Wendon Café.
Grid ref. 523 824 (Ordnance Survey Explorer 263).

The walk

1. Walk north (left as you face the sea) along the water front and take the signed coastal path on the right opposite the road 'Ffordd Cynlas'. This quickly climbs onto the sea cliffs overlooking the bay and is well used and easily followed.

These cliffs rise to almost 100 feet in places and the path passes quite close to the edge so care is needed here and there. The prominence of these sea cliffs may have given Benllech its name which means 'head of the rock' from the words 'pen' and 'llech'.

Further along the coast the rock scenery includes examples of features known as 'wave-cut platforms'. These take the form of flat rock platforms exposed at low tide. They are formed by wave erosion removing the upper rock layers and occur where sedimentary rocks—in this case limestone—retain their original horizontal layering. Other examples can be seen at the eastern end of Red Wharf Bay.

The path is well maintained and for most of the way is overhung by vegetation with only occasional glimpses of the cliffs below. Carry on along the coast to the end of the little

41

headland known as Penrhyn which looks out over the bay at Traeth Bychan (*little beach*).

Here you have a good view north across the cove of Traeth Bychan to the village of Moelfre. You will also see, if the tide is low, one of the largest wave-cut platforms on this part of the coast.

2. From the end of the headland continue along the edge of the rocks and pass several small holiday chalets. Beyond these drop to a tarmac access path heading down to the beach and turn left up the hill (coastal footpath). At the top of a short rise bear right onto an enclosed footpath (sign) with caravans to the left. A gate

Traeth Bychan from Penrhyn

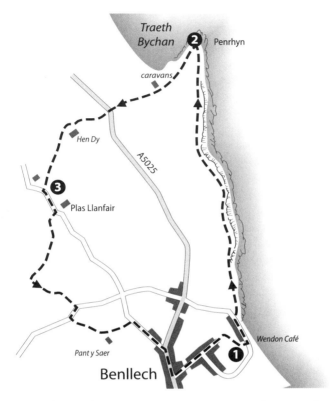

at the end of the path takes you onto a tarmac drive with a house to the right. Walk past the house ignoring the coastal path sign on the right, keeping ahead up the drive to the road.

Cross the road and walk down the access track to 'Hen Dy' directly opposite. Immediately before the farmyard, turn right to a stile which leads onto a short enclosed footpath with a stream to the right. At the end of the footpath cross a stile into fields and keep along the right-hand field edge (ignore a stile on the right here) to a stile in the far corner. Walk ahead through the following fields until you reach the garden of a bungalow. Go over a stile in the corner then turn left immediately through a gate into the garden. Keep left around the garden edge, then bear left up the bank as indicated to reach the lane.

3. Turn left along the lane and look for a signed footpath on the right opposite a house 'Plas Llanfair'. Turn right over the stile, cross a caravan site access road and go straight ahead between hedges to a tarmac footpath below overhead power lines. Turn left along the edge of the caravan field to cross a stile over the fence. Go straight ahead to a second stile by a large gate then ahead through the following caravan field keeping to the right of centre to a stile and stone steps over a stream in the far hedge.

In the following field, ignore a path (kissing gate) immediately on the left, instead, walk ahead to a kissing gate in the wall (approx 25 yards away). Go through the kissing gate and go ahead through the following field veering right to the outside corner of a large cottage garden. Bear right beside the garden to join a wooden walkway. Follow this to cross a footbridge over the stream and bear left up the following field to a kissing gate. Go through the kissing gate and turn left along a footpath to pass a house on the left ('Tŷ Mawr'). Bear right down the drive to the road.

Take the access road almost opposite signed to 'Pant y Saer Farm'. Walk down the road passing caravans on the right and just before the farmhouse, a sign and steps on the left take you into fields again. Walk through the field to a kissing gate in the lower right-hand corner and directly through the following field to the road. Turn right along the road and continue to the junction with the A5025 near 'Plas Glanrafon Hotel'. Turn right here and after about 200 yards turn left into 'Bay View Road'. At the bottom of the hill turn right through a kissing gate after the last house and follow the path through an area of gorse. Keep right at a fork and drop into the car park beside the 'Wendon

Moelfre

Distance: *4½ miles*

An easy walk along a popular section of coastal path and quiet country lanes. Footpaths are excellent throughout.

The walk visits the historic sites of Din Lligwy Iron Age village, the Lligwy Burial Chamber and the site of the wreck of the **'Royal Charter' (1859).**

Start: Begin the walk at the beach car park, Traeth Lligwy. *Grid ref. 497 871 (Ordnance Survey Explorer 263).*

The walk

1. From the car park turn right along the coastal path which is well defined and gives a fine view of the wide sweep of Traeth Lligwy with Ynys Dulas beyond. The first cove—Porth Forllwyd—is private and the path takes you beside a wall around the bay, before the path rejoins the coast to run along a series of low limestone cliffs.

On the approach to the small shingle inlet of Porth Helaeth, look to your right where a small stone memorial commemorates the wreck in 1859 of the 'Royal Charter': *'This stone commemorates the loss of the steam clipper* 'Royal Charter' *which was wrecked on the rocks nearby during the hurricane of 26th October 1859 when over 400 persons perished. Erected by public subscription in 1935.'*

The memorial overlooks the rocks where the ship was pounded to pieces and can be approached by a short field path on the right, just before the beach.

In its day, the 'Royal Charter' *was one of the fastest clippers on the run between Liverpool and Australia and her captain, Thomas Taylor,*

The tiny village of Moelfre

was justly proud of her. On August 26th 1859, she left Melbourne laden with a valuable cargo of gold and passengers who had made their fortune in the Australian goldfields. Eight weeks later she was almost within sight of Liverpool after a journey of over 16,000 miles when one of the worst storms of the century (which claimed a total of 133 ships and almost 800 lives, over half in this one tragedy) drove her onto rocks little more than a stone's throw from here. There were survivors, but very few; 465 lives were lost. The whole country was shocked by the disaster, particularly by the fact that no women or children were among the survivors and by rumours that locals had plundered bodies washed ashore in the days that followed.

The dead were buried locally in the cemeteries of several nearby villages and Rev. Stephen Hughes, of Llanallgo is said to have written over 1,000 letters to the families and friends of those who perished. So traumatic was the event and its aftermath that it is said to have brought about Rev. Hughes early death at the age of 47. He is buried in the little cemetery at Llanallgo where a memorial to him can be seen.

One survivor, by the name of James Dean, was not only lucky enough to be one of the few washed ashore alive, but also managed to keep hold of his fortune which he held in the form of a banker's draft wrapped in oilskin. He is said to have returned to Moelfre on the anniversary of the disaster for the remaining 36 years of his life to give thanks for his survival. His descendants carried on the practice for more than a century after the sinking.

Beyond the cove, the footpath rises to a caravan site then bears left to continue along the coast to open land on a small headland with Ynys Moelfre ahead across the narrow channel of Y Swnt. Further along, a signpost directs you onto a small shingle beach by cottages and at the far end you are directed right immediately before a cottage. Follow the path past the lifeboat station and Seawatch Centre, which houses an exhibition of sea rescue, along with the RNLI lifeboat *'Bird's Eye'*.

This craft was presented to the RNLI by Birds Eye Foods Ltd. and was used for over 20 years between 1970 and 1990 in New Quay. It was launched 89 times and saved 42 lives.

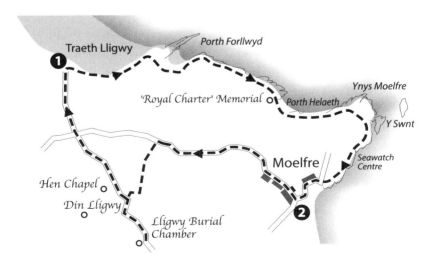

Beyond the Seawatch Centre, the path bears right to Moelfre harbour. Join the road here and turn left along the front, then up the hill passing the 'Kinmel Arms' on the right and the anchor taken from the wreck of the *'Hindlea'*, lost on October 27th 1959 almost 100 years to the day after the loss of the *'Royal Charter'* and in almost the same location.

2. Take the first road on the right and continue for approximately ¾ mile.

Immediately after the entrance to quarry workings on the left, turn left through a kissing gate onto a signed path. Rise to a second kissing gate and follow the right of way ahead along field edges. In the far corner of the second field, turn right along the field edge to a quiet lane.

Turn left here and follow the lane for about 300 yards to visit the Lligwy Burial Chamber which lies in fields to the right.

The most obvious feature of this burial chamber is the massive capstone: over 18 feet long and nearly 16 feet wide. It is estimated to weigh some 25 tons and was probably lifted into place with the aid of timber scaffolding. Two thirds of the chamber lie below ground level and make use of a natural fissure in the rock giving the chamber a very squat appearance. The entrance faces east towards the lane and originally the whole structure would have been covered by a mound of earth and stones which has been eroded away.

Excavations in 1909 revealed the unburnt remains of up to 30 individuals, as well as animal bones and pottery. The form and decoration of the pottery suggest that the chamber was in use during the late Neolithic and early Bronze Age periods.

Retrace your steps along the road passing the spot where you entered the lane. Beyond this, look for the signed footpath to 'Din Lligwy' and 'Hen Capel' on the left. The path keeps beside the fence on your left with the ruins of Hen Capel to your right. A metal kissing gate takes you into a small wood where a short rise leads to Din Lligwy.

Din Lligwy is one of the most remarkable and best preserved British settlements in the country and is thought to date from the middle of the fourth century, a period when the Romans were withdrawing from North Wales.

It is thought to have been the dwelling of a local chieftain or ruler and consists of a total of nine buildings; seven rectangular and two circular, which would originally have been thatched. The entrance is at the eastern end and a defensive wall some five feet thick surrounds the site which covers about half an acre. The two circular buildings are thought to have been dwellings, the rectangular huts were most likely barns or workshops.

Retrace your steps to the lane passing Hen Capel standing alone and isolated in the fields overlooking the bay.

Hen Capel or 'Old Chapel' dates from the twelfth century when most early Celtic churches were built in stone for the first time. By this period, Anglesey was finally free from the fear of Viking raids and the lower parts of the walls survive from this time. The upper half of the walls were built 200 years later and additions were also made in the sixteenth century. Inside, the walls were originally rendered although little remains today.

Turn left along the lane and at the crossroads go straight ahead returning to point 1.

Hen Capel

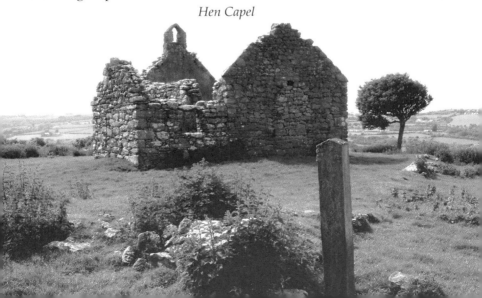

Traeth Ora and Mynydd Bodafon

Distance: *3¾ or 6½ miles*

A long walk centred on one of the most attractive beaches on this side of the island, with the option to include the excellent viewpoint of Mynydd Bodafon.

Start: Begin at the beach car park, Traeth Lligwy. This lies at the end of a narrow lane running northwest from the A5025 at Brynrefail, between Moelfre and Amlwch.
Grid ref. 492 873. (Ordnance Survey Explorer 263).

The walk

1. From the car park follow the signed coastal path to the left (when facing the sea) which runs north to the small sand and shingle beach of Porth-y-Môr (½ mile).

Immediately ahead you can see the rocks of Ynys Dulas, which lie a mile or so offshore. The prominent tower which can be seen, was built in 1824 as a beacon to identify the treacherous reef, of which the island is only a small part. The tower once incorporated a refuge for shipwrecked sailors and was kept stocked with food and provisions.

Walk ahead along the beach (ignore a stile on the left) and then continue on the obvious coastal path to Traeth Ora, a beautifully secluded sandy cove which cannot be approached by road. There is a kissing gate, a bench and a waymarker post immediately above the beach here.

(A footpath leads ahead through the bracken to the far end of the bay and the little headland which encloses the tidal eastuary of Traeth Dulas. It is a beautifully secluded spot and is well worth a visit, but you must return to this point to continue the walk.)

To continue, turn left on the well worn footpath (right if you took the detour to the end of the bay) which rises to Penrhyn farm. Turn right at the farm onto an access track and follow it to join a tarmac lane. Continue straight ahead up the lane and immediately before the first bend turn right onto a signed footpath around the garden of a cottage to enter fields through a kissing gate on the left.

Walk ahead up the gently sloping field with the sands and marshes of Traeth Dulas down to the right. Near the top of the field look for a squat

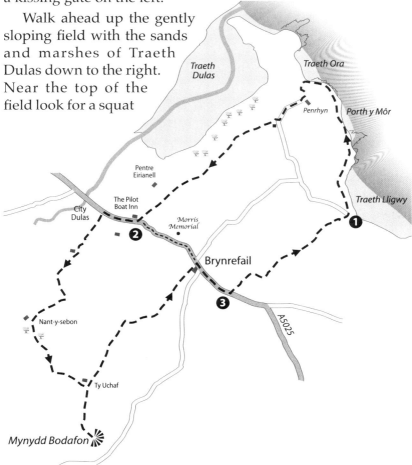

waymarker post on the left which directs you half-left through a gap in the hedge. At the time of writing there is a fenced enclosure on the other side of the hedge. Go ahead (to the right of the fenced enclosure) to the corner by an overgrown wall, then turn right between the fence and wall. At the end of the fence keep along the left-hand side of the field to cross a ladder stile and continue ahead, diverting around a pond if neccessary, to a gate and ladder stile in the far left corner leading onto a farm track. Follow the track for about 300 yards, and where this bears right, go through a kissing gate directly ahead into fields once more. Walk ahead along the right-hand field edge to the 'Pilot Boat Inn' (open all day at the time of writing).

2. Turn right down the hill passing the signed coastal footpath on the right. Just after the 'City Dulas' sign and before houses, take the signed footpath on the left. Follow the right of way along the left-hand field edge with Mynydd Bodafon directly ahead. At an access track turn right and follow it towards a bungalow. Go through a small gate on the left immediately before the bungalow and follow a path around the garden to a footbridge and stile into fields. Turn right and walk along the field edge to a stile and ahead again in the following field beside the stream.

At a shallow ditch separating two fields turn left and walk beside it. At the top of the field turn right over a footbridge and immediately left over a stile. Go right now on a good path to a footpath junction with ruins on the right.

Go ahead here over a stile, cross a footbridge over the stream and turn left immediately up the bank with the stream on your left. Higher up bear right to cross a ladder stile on the left. Go ahead along the left-hand edge of the following fields to a ladder stile on the left in a field corner. Cross the stile and walk beside the right-hand fence in the following fields to a farm. Immediately before the outbuildings go through a gate on the right and follow the access track as it curves left to a junction of tracks by 'Tŷ Uchaf'.

Turn right here and follow the obvious footpath which heads directly across the open heather covered hillside heading directly for the triangulation pillar on the summit of Mynydd Bodafon. As you approach the top bear left to the summit.

Although it rises to a modest 584 feet, this little hill gives a fine panorama over Anglesey's predominantly flat landscape. Out to the west you can see Holyhead Mountain and Mynydd y Garn along with the collection of wind farms near Cemaes Bay. Nearer at hand you have the spoil heaps of Parys Mountain, where copper has been mined since prehistoric times, and Mynydd Eilian with its two masts. Out to the east you will be able to see Puffin Island near Penmon Head along with the wide mouth of Red Wharf Bay and the blunt headland of the Great Orne near Llandudno on the skyline.

To the south, the interior of the island is rather featureless although the basic structure—a series of shallow valleys running northeast to southwest, can plainly be seen. It is one of these valleys which—now flooded—forms the Menai Strait separating Anglesey from the mainland. A second valley running between Malltraeth and Red Wharf Bay almost divides the island in two, although much of it has now been reclaimed.

Traeth Dulas

Back towards the mainland, the peaks of Snowdonia fill the southern skyline; from the rounded whale back slopes of the Carneddau in the east, to the sculptured pinnacles of Tryfan and Crib Goch on Snowdon. Further west, the isolated hills of the Lleyn Peninsula stand plainly on the farthest skyline.

Retrace you steps back to the junction of tracks at 'Tŷ Uchaf' and take the track directly ahead. Pass cottages on the left and go over the stile by the gate to 'Cae'r Mynydd' directly ahead. Walk through the garden to steps into fields again. Walk ahead to a stile in the corner of the first field then ahead through a large field to stiles and a footbridge. Keep ahead again to a stile into a rough area of gorse. A good path leads ahead through the gorse to a stile over the wall by rocks on the right. Keep to the right-hand edge of the fields and about 100 yards after the fence on the right ends, turn left across the field to pass beside a narrow woodland on the left. Drop down the bank and go through a kissing gate on the left. Turn right along the fenced wall to the corner of the field and climb steps over the wall near a bungalow on the right. Walk through a small field to a gate into the lane and turn left to Brynrefail.

3. Turn right along the A5025 and after about 500 yards, look for a signed footpath on the left which leads into fields. Go through the gate and walk ahead along field edges. Ignore a signed 'Permissive Path' keeping straight ahead and in the following field, immediately before a large house, turn right though a kissing gate. Follow the path beside the garden to a kissing gate in the bottom corner on the left. Go through the gate onto a drive beside the gateway to 'Siop y Rhos' and turn right down the drive. Almost immediately, where this turns right, go left over a stile and ahead along the edge of the field to cross a second stile. Follow a footpath between hedges to a farm on the right. Go ahead past the farm and through a large narrow field to a stile in the far hedgeline. This leads onto a path through gorse hedges to join a track. Turn left and follow the track back to the beach car park to complete the walk.

Llaneilian

Distance: *7¾ miles*

A moderate walk along a recently opened section of the coast in the extreme northeast corner of Anglesey. Some careful route finding will be required until the new coastal path becomes more established.

Start: There is a small free car park at Porth Eilian just before the cove and on the lane out to the lighthouse.
Grid ref. 477 929 (Ordnance Survey Explorer 263).

The walk

1. Turn right out of the car park and follow the lane down to the turning area by the sheltered cove of Porth Eilian. Bear right along the narrow lane which leads out to the lighthouse, situated at the end of the headland at Point Lynas (alternative car park here). Where the road bends left towards the lighthouse you will see the signed coastal path on the right. If you decide to walk out to the lighthouse, return to this point to continue the walk.

This long, finger-like headland has posed a threat to Liverpool bound shipping for over two centuries. The first beacon was built here in the early eighteenth century but the present lighthouse dates from 1835.

To continue, go through the kissing gate and follow the signed coastal path along the edge of a rough grazing field to a second kissing gate. Continue ahead by the wall for a few yards to the corner, then bear right through a large open field. As you pass under power lines the path splits. Take the right-hand fork across the field to a kissing gate in the wall by a rocky inlet. Go through the kissing gate and rise to another kissing gate. In the next field the path splits again—don't head for the kissing gate visible up to the right, follow the path left then bear left again before the fence on the obvious path. This path has recently been opened to up give access to the coast between here and the Dulas estate, previously out of bounds as no right of way existed.

The path is well used and marked frequently by waymarker posts as it contours through the bracken and gorse to stiles. Further on a footbridge leads over a stream and the path heads through more open grazing fields near the top of the coastal slope. Follow marker posts over into the next cove.

At Porthygwichiad the path makes a gradual drop through smaller fields to cross a footbridge. Aim for a ladder stile ahead which marks the continuation of the path. Keep ahead parallel to the wall on the right until you are directed half-left by a waymarker to the edge of the coast again.

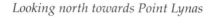

Looking north towards Point Lynas

As you round the next broad headland you are treated to a wide view along the east coast to Moelfre, Penmon and the mountains on the mainland. Also visible is Ynys Dulas with its curious tower.

Continue ahead close to field edges on the left above the next cove (Porth Helygen). Rise to a stile (ignore the path on the right) and keep to the left edge in the following field. Cross a footbridge and in the next field corner turn right up the field edges ahead lined by trees. Continue up the field edges ahead until a stile leads into an enclosed track. Walk ahead along the track to the road by a house on the right.

2. Turn right and walk along the lane to the first turning on the left (about ¾ mile). Turn left here and look for a signed footpath adjacent to 'Bryn Môr'. Walk ahead through the centre of the field to pass through a gateway and continue ahead again below overhead cables to enter a lane in the far corner. Turn right along the lane.

In about ½ mile there is a T junction with a wider road. About 50 yards before this there is a signed footpath on the right which can be used to reach the triangulation pillar on Mynydd Eilian. Return to the T junction to continue the walk.

From this high point you have a grand view of the northeastern corner of Anglesey. South and east, the view takes in the Dulas Estuary and Moelfre with Red Wharf Bay and Penmon lighthouse in the distance. Over on the mainland, the mountains of Snowdonia, along with the Great Orme and the Clwydian Range are also visible. In exceptionally clear conditions, you should be able to see the Isle of Man, the fells of the Lake District, the Lancashire coast and the mountains of southern Ireland.

Turning west, much of Anglesey's rugged northern coast is visible—from the lighthouse at Point Lynas past the harbour at Amlwch and the nuclear power station at Wylfa, to The Skerries on the extreme northwestern tip of the island. Further south, Holyhead Mountain can be seen along with the chimney of the aluminium works. In the far distance, the hills of the Lleyn Peninsula can just be seen over Anglesey's flat interior. Nearer at hand are the disfigured slopes of Parys Mountain, where copper has been mined since prehistoric times.

Turn right at the T junction and in about 200 yards, (immediately after a large bungalow 'Craig Lwyd') turn left onto a signed footpath. Follow the path through a small field

Point Lynas

and over a stile. Turn left along the footpath beside the wall at first, then curve right through a large field aiming just to the right of the distant power station and wind farms on the skyline. Cross a stone stile in the far corner of the field and follow the path through gorse bushes and a smaller field to a quiet lane at Pengorffwysfa.

Turn right and walk down the hill until the lane forks. Turn sharp left here on a signed footpath. Make your way through the centre of the field towards 'Henblas', a large farmhouse immediately ahead. Adjacent to the house cross a stile, then a second stile on the right which leads into the yard. Walk down the drive away from the house to the road.

3. Turn right along the lane. At Llaneilian church, bear left towards the gate leading into the cemetery and just before the gate, turn left up steps over the wall. Shortly, a gate leads into a farmyard. Walk ahead to a second gate to join a concrete farm track. Follow the track and where this bends right, bear left down the bank to join the coastal path.

For a short detour to Ffynnon Eilian, turn left and continue to the next inlet. As you drop down to the stream, look to your left where a large rock lies beside the stream and to the left of this, a second large rock has a spring bubbling from beneath it.

Ffynnon Eilian is the well of Saint Eilian and remnants of a drystone wall enclosure can still be seen at the foot of the large rock from which the water flows. The well is said to run water long into a dry spell even when the nearby stream has dried up.

The well is also reputed to have been used as a cursing well by the locals. The recipient's name was written on a small tablet of stone and dropped into the water. The curse was thought to remain as long as the stone remained in the well.

Return along the coastal path to Porth Eilian. At the road turn right up the hill to return to point 1.

Llaneilian derives its name from Saint Eilian who is said to have landed at nearby Porthyrychen with his cattle and possessions in the sixth century and established the first church here. According to local legend, he obtained the land for his church from Caswallon Law Hir (Caswallon The Long Handed), a nearby lord whom he struck with blindness for some misdemeanour. Caswallon was later forgiven, his sight restored and out of gratitude (or fear!) he promised Eilian a piece of land to establish his church.

Bull Bay

Distance: *4¼ miles*

A moderate, gentle walk on a quiet section of the coast; only in the approach to Bull Bay are you likely to meet other walkers. There are some interesting industrial remains at Porth Wen but they are in a derelict condition and are best viewed from a distance.

Start: Take the A5025 west from Amlwch and pass through Bull Bay. After about 2 miles, turn right into a narrow lane and in ½ mile or so, just beyond a farm on the left, park on the verge beside two signed footpaths on the right.
Grid ref. 398 943 (Landranger 114, Explorer 262).

The walk

1. Take the first of the two signed footpaths (when approaching from the A5025). Go ahead through the first field to a kissing gate and bear half-right through the following field to a second kissing gate. In the third field go ahead again aiming a little to the right of a distant farmhouse seen across the bay. Keep just to the right of rocks at the far side of the field and go through an old kissing gate. Pass through an area of gorse, bearing left down the bank. Turn right passing a squat waymarker post (where you join the coastal path) and cross a footbridge over a stream. Go through a kissing gate and walk ahead through the following field towards the farmhouse seen earlier.

Pass the farmhouse on the right and follow the access road. Where this bends right almost immediately, go ahead on the signed coastal path. Walk along a short grass track which soon opens out into a large field. Follow the visible coastal path which

The wide rocky bay of Porth Wen

keeps to the lower left edge of large open grazing fields. Take care near the may rocky inlets along this stretch.

Porth Wen is a wide unfriendly bay lined with steep cliffs and impressive rock scenery. With only a small beach to absorb the impact of winter storms, the slaty rock has weathered into a series of jagged narrow inlets which cut in towards the path.

On the far side of the bay you will see the abandoned remains of Porth Wen Brickworks with its tall chimneys and distinctive beehive shaped kilns. This enterprise used quartzite from nearby Craig Wen to make silica bricks for use in the steel industry. These were exported by boat from the little quay which can be seen adjacent to the works.

The existence of quartzite here probably gave the bay its name: Porth Wen means 'white port' and Craig Wen, from where the crystal was taken, means 'white crag' or 'white rock'.

Between here and Bull Bay the coastal path is well used and easily followed along the low cliffs and easy angled coastal slope. It becomes even better established as you near Bull Bay.

2. As you approach Bull Bay there are two kissing gates adjacent to one another. Go through the gate ahead which takes you on to a footpath around the little headland which encloses the cove.

At a tarmac access road by a house ('Craig y Wylan'), go ahead along the road and in about 50 yards turn left through a kissing gate. Follow the narrow footpath with gardens to the right (bay to the left) to the road by the 'Bull Bay Hotel' on the right.

Out to the east of Bull Bay you will be able to see the little rock of East Mouse or Ynys Amlwch. It was on this rock that the huge steam ship 'Dakota', one of the largest steamships to be wrecked on the Anglesey coast, ran aground and became a total wreck in 1877. The 'Dakota' was almost 400 feet long and built for speed to cover the transatlantic crossing—a feature which led to her downfall. The ship was outward bound for New York and just a few hours into the journey when the order was given to turn away from the coast. For reasons which have never been fully explained, the ship turned the wrong way and headed straight for the treacherous northern coast of the island. By the time the error was realised it was too late: the ship

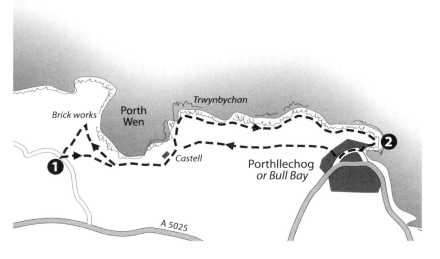

hit the rock and became a total wreck. All 218 passengers were rescued by the Bull Bay lifeboat but the reason for the helmsman's error remains a mystery.

Take the road opposite and walk up the rising lane past the toilets. Adjacent to a row of houses on the right almost at the top of the rise, turn right down the 'Private Road to Bryn Arthur and St Eleth'. Just before the house ('Bryn Arthur'), where the road bends right, bear left onto a signed footpath which leads into fields. Turn left, then bear right through the field to a stile beside a metal gate which leads onto a track. Turn right along the track and look for an iron kissing gate in the wall on the left just before a farmhouse ('Ty Gwyn'). Cut directly through two small fields to join a second access road with a house to the right. The right of way continues opposite, where a gate leads into fields once more. Keep right around the field edge and almost in the top corner of the field go through a gap in the ruined wall on the right.

Walk ahead a few paces then turn left up towards a small stone pillar and go through a gap in the wall. Follow the crest of a rocky rounded rib ahead keeping to the highest ground until the wide bay of Porth Wen comes into view. As you start to descend look for a kissing gate in the far left-hand corner of the field. Go through the kissing gate and keep ahead along the field edge beside the wall. Stay beside the wall as it bends leftwards to eventually join the short grass track used earlier (by the stone farmhouse).

Retrace your steps past the farmhouse and through the following fields crossing the footbridge over the stream. Pass the squat waymarker post and bear right along the lower edge of the field immediately backing the bay. Cross the stile in the top corner of the field and go ahead to a second stile. Cross this and go ahead again to a T junction with a broad path/track. Turn left and follow this path back to the lane to complete the walk.

Penmom Lighthouse and Puffin Island (walk 2)

Porth Eilian and Point Lynas Lighthouse (walk 8)

On Dinas Gynfor near Cemaes Bay (walk 10)

Sea pink, or thrift, can be seen all along the coastline

Yellow flag iris flourishes across Anglesey's damp areas

Approaching Hen Borth (walk 11)

Looking north from Ynys Fydlyn to The Skerries (walk 13)

Ellin's Tower, near South Stack (walk 15)

The beach, Cymyran (walk 17)

The coastal path, near Rhosneigr (walk 19)

Walking around the headland of Mynydd Mawr (walk 19)

Field path to Porth Cwyfan (walk 20)

Newborough Forest (walk 21)

Walking along the edge of Newborough Warren (walk 22)

Cemaes Bay

Distance: *5½ miles*

An excellent walk along a wild and dramatic section of the coast. Footpaths are adequate but a short section crosses an exposed coastal slope which some may find intimidating, particularly in wet or windy conditions. It is thus not recommended for small children or those nervous in such terrain.

Start: There is a small car park with WC facilities near the harbour in the village of Cemaes Bay.
Grid ref. 373 935 (Ordnance Survey Explorer 262).

The walk

1. From the car park, proceed eastwards along the seawall to a second car park at the end of a narrow lane. From here, turn left onto National Trust land at Penrhyn Mawr and follow the footpath which quickly climbs onto the low cliffs overlooking the bay.

From a viewpoint on the left you will see both the old and the new. For almost two centuries man has tried to harness one of Anglesey's most abundant energy resources — the wind. The little white towers of early windmills on the outskirts of the town are now dwarfed by the giant blades of the modern wind farms which turn slowly on the exposed hillside behind the village.

A good footpath weaves along field edges to Porth Padrig, Cemaes most easterly sandy beach and too far from local facilities to be overcrowded. Here you can make a short detour onto the sand or bear right to where a kissing gate leads into a quiet lane. Turn left now and follow the lane to the tiny church of Saint Badrig.

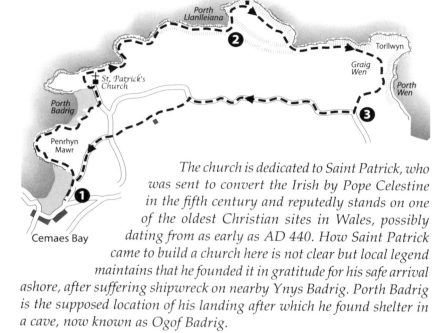

The church is dedicated to Saint Patrick, who was sent to convert the Irish by Pope Celestine in the fifth century and reputedly stands on one of the oldest Christian sites in Wales, possibly dating from as early as AD 440. How Saint Patrick came to build a church here is not clear but local legend maintains that he founded it in gratitude for his safe arrival ashore, after suffering shipwreck on nearby Ynys Badrig. Porth Badrig is the supposed location of his landing after which he found shelter in a cave, now known as Ogof Badrig.

The present building is a small structure, just 60 feet by 14 feet and stands on the very edge of the cliffs, defying the frequent winter gales which sweep in from the Irish Sea. It is mainly of sixteenth century construction although sections of the interior may date from medieval times.

In 1884 it was restored by Lord Stanley of Alderley, whose work showed the influence of his recent conversion to the Muslim faith. Much of this was destroyed by fire in 1985, although recent renovation has allowed it to be open to the public once more.

Beyond the church, the cliffs turn eastwards and the walk becomes considerably more rugged. Bear left by the church gate and at the end of the wall turn right onto the cliff path which skirts the walled cemetery overlooking the sea. Follow this until you are directed left near a wire fence ahead.

Go through a kissing and keep close by the fields on your right as you are very close to large cliffs on the left. After steps you curve rightwards again before rising once more. Just before the top of the next rise, a narrow footpath curves left across the middle of the slope.

You will need a sure foot and a steady head to traverse these slopes, particularly in wet and or windy conditions and some may find this section very intimidating. This is no place to allow adventurous children to wander! Don't be tempted to seek what appears to be easier ground higher up the slope, this will only lead you into greater difficulties.

Soon the headland of Dinas Gynfor and Porth Llanlleiana come into view and the angle eases. Ahead, a final pointed knoll forces you either ahead along more exposed slopes or to the right through bracken to a stone wall. Both options lead shortly to the ruins at Porth Llanlleiana.

These ruins are one of the many relics from Anglesey's industrial past which dot this now deserted coastline. In addition to the crumbling buildings there are traces of a small port used to export locally dug china clay.

2. Behind the ruins, a footpath strikes out diagonally to the left up the steep hillside. Although quite steep, the toil is soon over and you are left with an easy stroll through heather and bracken to another ruined building; the old lookout on Dinas Gynfor, Wales' most northerly headland.

The lookout is well sited. From here you can see almost the entire northern coast, from Point Lynas in the east to The Skerries off Carmel Head. Between lies some of the wildest and most unspoilt coastline on the island.

The defensive possibilities of Dinas Gynfor were exploited in prehistoric times when the summit was enclosed to form a fortress some 700 yards by 300 yards. The site was well chosen, even today the high plateau is only approachable with ease at its eastern end where the coastal path drops to Porth Cynfor.

From the lookout, an easy path leads through the heather

Ruins at Porth Llanlleiana

before dropping steeply to Porth Cynfor (Hell's Mouth). Ahead, steps lead back to clifftop level and the angle eases once more.

Ahead you will see the old winding gear from Porth Wen Brickworks situated lower down on the hillside. Further along, the crumbling chimneys and kilns overlook Porth Wen, a wide picturesque bay which marks the eastern limit of our walk. Today these enterprises seem strangely out of place in such otherwise unspoilt terrain, yet there are many such relics as we have already seen at Llanlleiana and we have our twentieth century counterpart in the form of nearby Wylfa Nuclear Power Station.

On a less grim note, the beacon mast to your left, situated on Torllwyn, is used by shipping, along with its counterpart on Porthllechog to the east, to determine an exact nautical mile.

Bear right a little further on and follow a good path above the ruins with a wide view of Porth Wen. Beyond a gate and kissing gate, the footpath continues to a quiet lane.

3. Turn right along the lane and continue for almost 1 mile.

After a bend and just before farm buildings ahead, a sign and stile indicate a field path on the left. Turn left here and cut through the centre of the field to a footbridge, then aim to the right of a farmhouse where stiles lead across the access track and into fields once more. Walk ahead and rise slightly to a kissing gate, then bear right to follow a well defined footpath ahead beside a wire fence. At the lane turn right, then after about 30 yards turn left and return along the lane to Cemaes Bay.

Looking east along the coast from Dinas Gynfor

Cemlyn Bay

Distance: *3½ miles*

A short easy walk along a section of gentle coastline which can be combined with the following route for a longer walk. An unusual beach formation and rich array of bird life add interest. Footpaths are excellent throughout.

Start: There is a car park and information board at the eastern end of Cemlyn Bay. This is approached via a narrow lane, which leaves the A5025 at Tregele opposite the 'Douglas Inn'. Under occasional very high tides the outflow from the lagoon which backs the beach can not be crossed, in which case cars can be parked and the walk started at the car park beside Bryn Aber at the western end of the bay *(Grid ref. 329 936).*
Grid ref. 336 932. (Ordnance Survey Explorer 262).

The walk

1. From the car park turn left (when facing out to sea) along the beach (Esgair Cemlyn).

The unusual formation of the beach has been caused by centuries of onshore winds, depositing stones and shingle across the mouth of the bay to form a ridge ('esgair'). This has created a brackish lagoon on the landward side fed by fresh water and inundated by the sea only on the highest tides. Water level in the lagoon is maintained by a weir at the far end of the beach, built in the 1930s and repaired in 1978.

The lagoon was managed as a private wildlife refuge for 40 years until the National Trust bought it with funds from Enterprise Neptune in 1971. The area is now leased by North Wales Wildlife Trust who maintain it as a nature reserve.

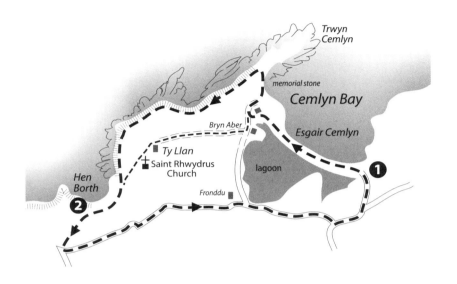

Unsurprisingly, the pool is a haven for wildlife and supports large numbers of grey mullet, along with a variety of wildfowl including: mallard, shelduck, redshank, oystercatcher, redbreasted merganser, coot, little grebe and tufted duck.

Of particular note is the tern colony, which is one of the largest in Britain and returns here each spring to breed. The reserve provides a unique opportunity to view a tern colony at such close quarters, although you are requested to follow the viewing instructions so as not to disturb birds during the breeding season. Please do not walk along the grass bank by the pool between April and July when the birds are nesting.

At the far end of the beach, cross a small concrete causeway which leads over the outlet stream from the lagoon (NB. during very high tides this may not be possible). Turn left now and walk over flat rocks beside a high wall and deserted farmhouse to a car park. Turn right along a gravel track which leads onto the National Trust land at Trwyn Cemlyn.

The tiny church of Saint Rhwydrus

On the way, there is a stone memorial on the right to commemorate the 150th anniversary of the first lifeboat on Anglesey (1828-1978). This was founded by the Reverend James Williams and his wife Frances after witnessing the wreck of the Irish Packet 'Alert' which drifted onto West Mouse killing 145 people in 1823. The Reverend and his wife are said to have watched helplessly from this headland as the packet ship sank, leaving only seven survivors.

James and Frances devoted the rest of their lives to the formation of the Anglesey Association for the Preservation of Life from Shipwreck. James was awarded the first RNLI Gold medal in Wales, after playing a major role in the rescue of sailors from the vessel 'Active', wrecked in Cemaes Bay in 1835. Ironically, it was not at the helm of his lifeboat but from the shore, where he used his horse to get deeper into the surf and throw a grappling iron to the wreck, thus saving the lives of five men.

Here you can either walk over rough grass to the end of the

headland for a view of the bay, or bear left following the wall to a corner overlooking flat wave-cut rocks, where a kissing gate leads into fields on your left. The path now keeps tight against the right-hand field boundary, overlooking the sea to your right.

At low tide there is a panorama of wave-cut platforms and small islands out towards The Skerries. On a blustery day, there is a strong Hebridean feel to this remote weather-beaten corner of Anglesey, which stands in sharp contrast to the softer south and east coasts.

These notorious reefs have been a hazard to shipping for centuries and caused the wreck in 1854 of the steamer 'Olinda' which hit Harry Furlough's Rocks and broke up. Fortunately, all those on board were rescued by the Cemlyn Lifeboat.

Continue along the coastal footpath passing above the little church of Saint Rhwydrus which can be seen down to the left. A public right of way leads back to the church from a kissing gate just before the next cove (Hen Borth) where a small shingle bank backs the bay.

Dedicated to Saint Rhwydrus, the simple form and plain interior of the church is typical of many early Celtic churches on Anglesey. The font and nave date from the twelfth century and the chancel dates from a century later. In the little cemetery surrounding the church there are a number of graves from the eighteenth and nineteenth centuries.

2. At the far end of the shingle beach cross a stream and turn left through a kissing gate. Walk along the field edge, go through a second kissing gate and follow the footpath beside the stream and over a small footbridge to the road. Turn left along the lane.

From the lane you can look left towards the little church and the bay at Hen Borth. The landscape on this part of the island is composed mainly of glacial drift and boulder clay, creating a series of hummocks or 'drumlins' covering the bedrock. This covering has been easily eroded by the sea, which can be seen to dramatic effect to the left of the church, where a drumlin has been cut almost in two at its highest point.

Keep straight ahead beyond the house 'Fronddu' ignoring

a left turn. At a T junction turn left and turn left again at a fork after about 300 yards. Walk along the lane back to the car park at point 1.

(Alternatively, from the beach at Hen Borth you can return along the coastal path and at the second kissing gate bear right across the field to the little church of Saint Rhwydrus. Pass to the left of the church and cemetery (where there are steps over the wall to visit the church) and walk towards the farmhouse directly ahead. Enter the farmyard and go ahead down the access road. At the end of the road turn left and retrace your steps along the beach.)

Heading west on the coastal path from Cemlyn Bay

Carmel Head

Distance: *4½ miles*

An excellent walk in the remote northwest corner of the island. The walking is gentle with views out to the famous Skerries. Footpaths are a little indistinct in places.

Start: There is a small National Trust car park (free) near the Mynachdy Estate. This is approached by following the lane to Cemlyn Bay but instead of turning right down the short lane which leads to the bay, take the next right. Where the lane bears right down to Trwyn Cemlyn after about ¼ mile, keep left. The car park is on the right after ¾ mile just before a sharp left-hand bend. *Grid ref. 317 926 (Ordnance Survey Explorer 262).*

The walk

1. Turn right out of the car park and go through the kissing gate immediately on the right, which leads onto the National Trust property at Mynachdy (information board). Follow the right of way over a small footbridge, and beside the stream. Go through a second kissing gate and keep ahead along the field edge to join the coastal footpath at a kissing gate at the little bay of Hen Borth.

Turn left here and follow the coastal path which hugs the edge of fields almost to Carmel Head where you will see the curious stone structures known as the 'White Ladies'—almost 2 miles.

This wild treacherous coastline lies on the busy shipping lane to Liverpool and has thus been a major hazard for centuries. This was particularly true during the age of sail, when numerous ships were driven onto its notorious reefs and islands by onshore winds. Ironically,

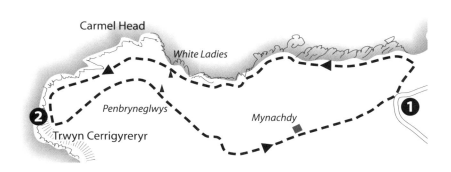

one of the most famous wrecks was caused by a lack of wind when the Irish Packet 'Alert' drifted onto West Mouse after running out of wind while rounding Carmel Head. The Reverend James Williams of nearby Llanfairynghornwy and his wife Frances watched helplessly as 145 people drowned. They were so distraught by the tragedy and their inability to help that they established the first lifeboat in Wales at Cemlyn in 1828.

Northwest of Carmel Head lies the group of rocks known as The Skerries—a Norse name derived from the word 'sker' meaning 'steep rock'. In Welsh they are known as Ynysoedd y Moelrhoniaid or 'Seal Islands' and were the scene in 1675 of the wreck of Britain's first Royal Yacht, the 'Mary' presented to Charles II. The remains of this ship were found by accident in 1971 in 40 feet of water.

Originally, The Skerries were owned by Bangor Cathedral but were diverted into private ownership by Bishop Nicholas Robinson during the 1570s. In 1713, the islands were leased by a descendant of the Bishop's to William Tench. He built the first beacon in 1716 and planned to collect duties from shipping entering Holyhead, however, the venture proved to be disastrous and he died penniless in 1725. Tragically, he also lost his son who drowned while ferrying coal to The Skerries to keep the beacon running. Another tragedy happened to a descendant of Bishop Robinson on the 20th June 1739, when William Robinson and twelve companions drowned while returning from the beacon. Their empty boat was washed ashore four days later at Whitehaven in Cumbria.

After a long and troubled history The Skerries became the last privately owned lighthouse in the country and was eventually sold for £444,984 11s 2d in 1841.

A rather curious wreck occurred at Carmel Head in the early 1740s, when an unknown vessel sank leaving two young boys as the only survivors. They came ashore lashed to a raft but as they could speak no Welsh or English, they could tell their rescuers nothing about the ship or its crew. One of the boys was adopted by a local family and given the name Evan Thomas. Evan eventually learned to speak Welsh and found that he had a gift for the setting of bones, which he later developed into a successful business. His descendants founded the Robert Jones and Agnes Hunt Orthopaedic Hospital near Oswestry. Nothing is known of the second youngster but both boys are assumed to have been Spanish.

Other links with shipping can be seen nearby in the form of the two large beacons known as the 'White Ladies'. These line up with a similar tower on West Mouse, to act as a guide for shipping negotiating Carmel Head.

At the White Ladies, the coastal path leaves the rocky coastal edge which swings rightwards to Carmel Head. Follow the coastal path ahead and slightly left marked by waymarker posts, to cross a footbridge over a ditch. Keep ahead passing a tall chimney associated with local mining and continue until Holyhead Mountain comes into view and you are forced to rise leftwards to a prominent rocky summit above the headland of Trwyn Cerrigyreryr.

From here there is a wide view of Holyhead Bay. To the southwest you will see the Irish ferries arriving and leaving Holyhead Harbour as they have done for centuries. Today however, this once hazardous and major undertaking can be completed quite safely in under two hours. Behind the town, Holyhead Mountain rises to over 800 feet, the highest point on the island. Further south the chimney at the aluminium works forms a prominent and well known landmark. On clear days, or just before sunset, you can often see the hills of southern Ireland on the western horizon. To the south, the coast becomes less dramatic beyond Church

The White Ladies

Bay, although the coves between Carmel Head and Porth y Bribys present some of the grandest sea cliff scenery on the island.

The wide panorama from this hilltop was first exploited by the Romans, who are thought to have built a beacon and lookout on the summit of nearby Penbrynyreglwys, to guard the entrance to their harbour at what is now Holyhead.

2. Head back towards the mine ruins (chimney) seen earlier. These are not visible yet and there are few trails to follow, so cut across the open hillside aiming just to the right of the beacon on West Mouse but keeping to the left of the rounded flat summit of Penbrynyreglwys, until the ruins come into view. The chimney is the first to be seen along with a view east along the north coast.

The mines date from a period of prosperity in the copper industry during the eighteenth century, although there is evidence of mining here in prehistoric times.

Pass between the ruins on your left and the chimney on the right and pick up a grass track which contours the hillside to a gate beyond the White Ladies beacons. Beyond the gate, follow the track through a larger grazing field to a gate and stone steps in the far corner. Bear half-right through a smaller field to a ladder stile about 150 yards away and head left along a track which soon curves to the right around a small artificial pool backed by conifer woods. Follow the track towards farm buildings at Mynachdy and pass through the farmyard to a gate immediately ahead. Go through the gate and follow the obvious track through grazing fields back to the lane and car park to complete the walk.

Until recent decades, access to this part of the coast was very restricted having few public rights of way. In 1986 the National Trust bought 412 acres of the Mynachdy Estate and have opened the area to the public, however, access to parts of the coast is only permitted between 1 February and 14 September. **Restrictions do not apply to this route.**

The Skerries and Trwyn Cerrigyreryr

Church Bay and Ynys y Fydlyn

Distance: *5 miles*

A beautiful walk visiting a remote rocky cove followed by a section of dramatic coastline. Moderately strenuous, on quiet lanes and good footpaths.

Start: Parking and WC facilities are available beside the beach café at Church Bay, signposted off the A5025 at Llanfaethlu. *Grid ref. 301 892 (Ordnance Survey Explorer 262).*

The walk

1. Turn left out of the car park and walk down the lane towards the beach. Just before the ramp down onto the sand, bear right onto the signed coastal footpath which backs the bay.

Where the path runs into fields beyond a gate, keep to the left-hand field edge, then in the second field cut diagonally-right to the top corner (the coastal footpath keeps left here). There are two cottages to the right here. Make your way up through the gorse bushes directly ahead and slightly right and higher up look for a stile (near power lines) and finger post in the wall and fence to your right. Cross the stile and turn left along an access track passing a cottage on the left.

Where the track bends sharp left with a wall ahead, turn right for a few yards to where stone steps below a finger post lead over the wall on the left. Go over the wall and bear half-left through the field to a stile on the external corner of a smaller field. Keep ahead to stone steps in the far corner of the field. Walk directly through

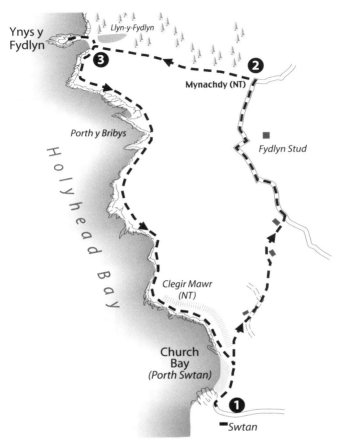

the centre of two larger fields in the direction of a farmhouse. Bear left around the farm and join a track which cuts through the following field to join a narrow track by a house and farm buildings on the left. Walk up to the lane and turn left. Follow the lane for about ¾ mile.

2. Where the lane bends sharp right, turn left onto a track which takes you onto National Trust land at Mynachdy (identified by a small sign, information panel and parking area).

In 1986 the National Trust bought 412 acres of the Mynachdy Estate with support from the Countryside Commission. This enabled a large

Ynys y Fydlyn

section of wild coastline to be opened to the public where previously
there had been few public rights of way.

Much of this land is now managed as a pheasant rearing area, with
a winter shoot providing the main income for the estate; because of this,
access to footpaths within the estate (restrictions do not affect this route)
is only permitted between 1 February and 14 September.

Follow the track beside conifer woods on the right down to
the beautiful little cove at Ynys y Fydlyn.

This little cove with its shingle beach, crystal clear water and fine
rock scenery is one of the most attractive locations on this part of the
island. The remoteness of the cove probably means that you will have it
to yourself, although you may be watched from the woods by thousands
of young pheasants specially bred for the winter shoot.

At low tide it is easy enough to get onto Ynys y Fydlyn, from where you will be able to enjoy a fine view of the dramatic rock scenery which surrounds the cove. To the north, there is a huge sea cave and a pool which backs the bay (known as Llyn y Fydlyn). This was once a small inlet from the sea but has now become separated. Both these features have been formed by the action of waves over the centuries, particularly during the winter months when strong westerly gales persist. Large sea caves like this can also be seen at North Stack on the exposed western coast of Holy Island.

Beyond Carmel Head, the lighthouse on The Skerries warns shipping of the treacherous rocks and reefs which grasp at ships passing Anglesey's northwestern tip. This coastline has been a hazard to shipping for centuries and has been responsible for literally hundreds of wrecks. One of the most notable was that of the 'Mary', a 52 foot sloop which sank after hitting the rocks in thick fog in 1675. The 'Mary' came from Amsterdam and was presented to Charles II, making it the first royal yacht. The 'Hudiksvall', a Swedish barque, was wrecked on Ynys y Fydlyn in 1890 and the crew of 116 were forced to lash themselves to the upper rails until the Holyhead Lifeboat came to their aid. All lives were saved.

3. Rise leftwards out of the bay to join the coastal footpath. The footpath is clear now although a little narrow in places and makes its way along the edge of the coastal slope.

At Porth y Bribys, cross a small stone bridge carrying a farm track and where this bends left almost immediately, take the footpath ahead. Follow the most obvious footpath along the coastal slope with broad views out over Holyhead Bay.

A section of permissive path cuts through fields marked by stiles, before joining the cliff edge once more at National Trust land ('Clegir Mawr').

Recent path improvements as you round the final headland before Church Bay make the final steep slopes easy and safe to negotiate. A kissing gate leads into fields above Church Bay and the outward journey can now be followed back to the car park.

Llanfachraeth

Distance: *6 miles*

An unusual walk on quiet lanes and along wide open beaches to the mouth of a small tidal estuary. Field paths lead back along the marsh edge to the village of Llanfachraeth. Easy level walking for much of the way.

Start: Begin the walk in the village of Llanfachraeth situated 3 miles north of Valley on the A5025. Park at the northern end of the village where there is a loop of the old road opposite the church. *Grid ref. 314 832 (Landranger 114, Explorer 262).*

The walk

1. Immediately opposite the lay-by and just past the large house beside the church turn left onto a signed footpath. This is enclosed at first with a high wall to the left. After about 50 yards a small gate on the right leads into a field. Walk directly through the field to enter a lane by a kissing gate and finger post. Turn left along the lane and walk for about 1 mile to Llanfwrog church.

Walk past the church on your left and after about 150 yards turn left into the signed lane to 'Penrhyn'. Ignore the lane on the right after about 500 yards ('Porth Tywyn Sandy Beach'), instead, continue along the road almost to the beach at Porth Penrhyn-mawr.

2. Here, within a hundred yards of the beach the road forks. Keep right on the concrete road for 100 yards or so before turning left across a small area of grass to join an unsurfaced track with a bungalow to the left. Follow this track along the back of the bay, then rise towards a farm.

84

Do not follow the track left into the farm, instead cross the stile straight ahead and walk directly up the following field. The next stile is not in the field corner but in the middle of the top hedge line. Keep left in the following field and walk down towards a farm on the edge of the next bay.

Despite a modest height of just 70 feet there is a fine view of the surrounding countryside from this little hill. To your right, across the wide sweep of Holyhead Bay the Irish ferries can be seen entering and leaving Holyhead harbour, whilst the chimney of the aluminium works provides one of the most visible landmarks on this side of the island. Directly ahead the distant peaks of Yr Eifl (The Rivals) can be seen on the horizon with the higher summits of Snowdonia further to the left.

Keep to the left of the farm passing through a gap in the hedge, then bear half-right to a ladder stile before outbuildings. Go through the gate here and turn left along the track. At the end of the track turn right at a T junction and walk down onto the beach. Turn left here and walk along the sand for almost 1 mile.

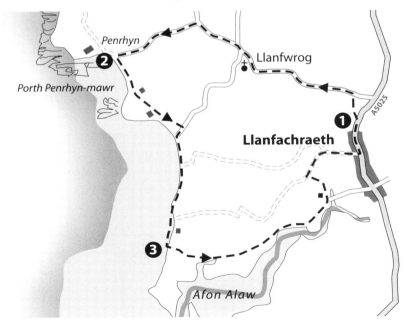

3. After passing a house almost on the sand, look for a stile and gate on the left (about 300 yards past the house). This leads onto a track which heads towards a ruined farm building. About 50 yards along the track turn right over a stile, then bear left along the edge of fields. The right of way is not visible on the ground initially, but cuts through an area of heather-covered sand dunes to an embankment used to prevent flooding of the fields to the left.

The name of nearby Llanfachraeth, which means 'church at the little beach or inlet', undoubtedly refers to this small tidal estuary where Afon Alaw enters the sea at Holyhead Bay.

Afon Alaw is linked in folklore to the sad story of Branwen, one of the collection of traditional Welsh stories known as the Mabinogion. The tale, which is though to date from about 1060, concerns Bran a Welsh prince and his beautiful sister Branwen. Bran is approached by the king of Ireland for the hand of his sister in marriage. The match is agreed between the two rulers and Branwen travels back to her new home in Ireland. Things do not go well for Branwen in Ireland though; the king turns against her on account of a trick played on him in Wales. She is imprisoned and forced to labour long hours in the kitchens. Despite all communication being cut with Wales she manages to get a letter to her brother at Caernarfon by means of a starling which she has trained during her ordeal. The result is war between Wales and Ireland and many battles are fought before Branwen is released.

Stepping once more onto Welsh soil here at the mouth of Afon Alaw with what remained of her brother's army (just seven knights!) she fell to her knees and declared, "woe is me that ever I was born: two good islands have been laid waste because of me!" With that she lay down and died of a broken heart. Her body was carried inland along the course of the river where a mound was raised over her grave.

In the fields near the outflow from Llyn Alaw five or six miles upstream from here a mound known as 'Bedd Branwen' or 'Branwen's Grave' can still be seen and is the supposed location of her burial. The mound is certainly of great antiquity, in fact it was already ancient when this story was written. In 1813 it was excavated and a Bronze Age urn with the remains of cremated bones found at its centre.

Cross a stile at the far end of the sea wall and bear half-left through the bracken. Aim just to the right of a small stone farm building and eventually pick up a faint track which will take you to a ladder stile on the left. Bear diagonally-left across the next field to the outside corner of a field on the left. There is a waymark here and a field to the right which is marshy and frequently inundated by high tides. Keep left along the field edge to a ladder stile which leads onto a short access track. After a few yards turn right over a second ladder stile and keep along the fence to a stile in the lower right-hand corner. This leads onto the marsh edge and may be flooded during certain high tides (if so either wait for the water to fall or return across the field and turn right to the lane. Follow this lane back to Llanfachraeth).

The path along the marsh edge stays close to the hedge and fence on your left. Further on a stile leads into a small field and a second stile takes you back onto the marsh edge again. Continue to a kissing gate beside a farm on the left. Turn right here then left immediately before the old bridge onto a signed footpath which runs beside a tidal pool on the right. Do not cross the stone footbridge over the pool, instead, continue straight ahead to stone steps over the wall which lead into a small field. Keep left to a stile in the corner and in the following field bear half-left to a stile and gate which lead into a narrow lane. Turn right and follow the lane to Llanfachraeth. A left turn here will take you back to the lay-by opposite the church.

Holyhead Mountain

Distance: *4½ miles*

A popular and spectacular walking area with the most dramatic cliff scenery on Anglesey and the island's highest point. Footpaths are good throughout

Start: A free car park is situated opposite the 'Hut Circle' sign almost at the end of 'South Stack Road'.
Grid ref. 210 819 (Ordnance Survey Explorer 262).

The walk

1. From the car park, follow the signed footpath to Ellin's Tower, 500 yards or so across the heather.

This tower was built as a summer retreat for Ellin, the wife of William Stanley in 1867. Ellin was a keen observer of the bird life to be found around South Stack and her husband, who was the liberal MP for Anglesey from 1837-74, was responsible for several archaeological excavations on Holyhead Mountain. During their lifetime, the couple also provided Holyhead with a hospital, a home for sailors, the Market Hall and the town's water supply. Ellin died in 1876 and her husband joined her eight years later.

Ellin's Tower became a popular attraction in the closing years of the nineteenth and early twentieth centuries, before falling into decay after World War II. In 1980 it was bought by the RSPB who carried out renovation work and opened it to the public as an information centre and bird hide in 1982.

Birds which can be seen here in large numbers include guillemots, which favour the crowded, narrow ledges, and puffins, often found on the steep grassy slopes above the cliffs. Other birds commonly seen include: fulmars, razorbills, shags, Manx shearwater and herring gull.

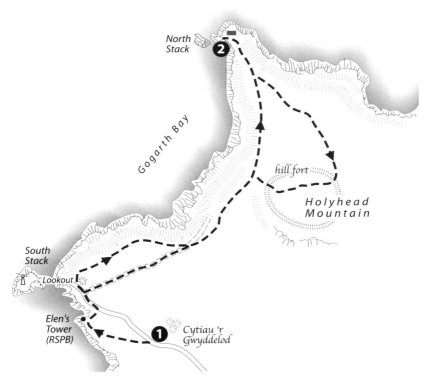

The cliff scenery directly below the tower and around the lighthouse at South Stack is amongst the most dramatic on Anglesey and a number of rock climbs have been recorded on the near vertical cliffs below the tower. During the nesting months however, there is a climbing restriction to prevent disturbance.

From Ellin's Tower, take the steps up the hill to the road and turn left. The path to South Stack lighthouse passes through a gateway at the end of the road. If you visit the lighthouse (fee required) return to this point to continue the walk.

If you do not visit the lighthouse, bear right onto the signed coastal footpath which rises to a ruined lookout building with commanding views of the surrounding coastline and a 'bird's eye view' of South Stack and the lighthouse.

South Stack Lighthouse

The ruins are the remains of the Holyhead Telegraph Station which stood at the western end of a chain of semaphore signalling stations linking Holyhead with Liverpool. It was installed by the Trustees of Liverpool Docks in 1827 and transmitted a message visually by means of movable arms. Although crude by modern standards, it was surprisingly effective when in use and in good conditions, could convey a simple message over a distance of 75 miles in just one minute.

Directly below, you will see South Stack lighthouse, built in 1808 to provide a vital warning for the Liverpool shipping lane and the Irish Packet service. It was automated in 1984.

Behind the lookout, an obvious path continues along the rocky crest of a rounded ridge with fine views ahead to North Stack and the massive cliffs of Gogarth, a popular but serious rock climbing area.

After passing small pools on the right the path drops a little, then rises to a narrow tarmac road (there are two small brick buildings over to the right here and 'dishes' to the left). Cross over and follow the prominent gravel footpath opposite which heads towards the crags of Holyhead Mountain.

Pass the 'dishes' on your left and at a fork keep left. At a second fork a little further on, keep right on the main path which clearly heads towards the shoulder of Holyhead Mountain (the path to the left is used to reach the rock climbing area at Gogarth). As you approach the shoulder, stone steps lead up the rise. At the top, bear left at a junction of paths and follow the coastal path over a small minor summit with ruined drystone walling at the highest point. From here drop more steeply down towards North Stack. Lower down, join a prominent broad path or track which swings in from the right and follow it down to North Stack.

Like South Stack, this rock has been separated from the mainland by the erosion of waves over thousands of years. If you walk down to the end of the rock opposite North Stack and look back, you will see a massive sea cave which will eventually create a stack out of the rock which you are now standing on. A number of high grade rock climbs have been recorded here and climbers can often be seen dotting the face to the right of the cave.

2. Retrace your steps up the hill on the broad path/track following power cables for a while. Don't turn back up the coastal path on the right (where you joined the broad path/track on the descent) instead, continue ahead for about 250 yards and just as the path begins to level, and immediately before it begins to drop, a narrower but obvious footpath curves to the right. Turn right onto this path and follow it as it rises through the heather. The path is narrow at first but it remains the most obvious path (ignore minor paths left and right) and can easily be followed.

Continue until you reach a level spot where the southwest coast of Holy Island around Trearddur comes into view ahead, with the hills of the Lleyn Peninsula beyond. Turn right at a junction of paths (before the path begins to drop) and follow the meandering footpath to the summit of Holyhead Mountain.

At the highest point on the island, this is a fine viewpoint with a spectacular panorama taking in almost the entire western side of Anglesey and Holy Island. To the north, you have the wide sweep of Holyhead Bay with The Skerries and Carmel Head in the far distance and the huge breakwater which shelters the harbour at Holyhead directly below. To the south and southeast, the view takes in the resorts and sandy bays of Trearddur, Rhoscolyn and Rhosneigr. On the horizon, the hills and rugged heights of Snowdonia stand above the flat green pastures of Anglesey's interior. Southwest, the hills of the Lleyn Peninsula can be picked out, with Bardsey in the far distance. In clear conditions, the Isle of Man and the hills of southern Ireland can often be seen.

This commanding view of the bay was evidently part of the attraction of the site to the Iron Age settlers who built the hillfort here, remains of which can still be seen. Throughout much of the Iron Age and the early post-Roman era, when this hillfort is thought to have been used, a major threat came from Irish tribes who sailed east to plunder the western coast of Britain.

The hillfort is known as Caer y Tŵr and extends over an area of 17 acres, making use of the hill's natural defences to the southeast and southwest. This is complemented by a wall around the northern perimeter some thirteen feet thick and still almost ten feet high in places. The entrance is at the northeast corner where the wall can be seen to turn inwards, forming an imposing passageway which could easily be defended.

Within the hillfort no hut circles have been identified, although the base of a Roman watchtower can be seen on the highest point next to the triangulation pillar. This was almost certainly linked to the Roman coastal fort at Caer Gybi (Holyhead) and is thought to have been used, along with a similar lookout on Penbrynyreglwys near Carmel Head, to guard the approaches to the fort and its harbour.

From the summit, take one of the paths which drop to the north (be careful of cliffs to the left) to join the path used earlier. Turn left down the steps and follow the gravel path back to the tarmac road beside the 'dishes'. Turn left here and follow the road back to the lane used earlier to reach South Stack. Turn left and return to the car park at point 1.

Opposite the car park entrance, a short path leads to a collection of prehistoric hut circles.

The site was originally excavated by William Stanley (who we have already mentioned in connection with Ellin's Tower) in the 1860s, when the remains of over 50 hut circles were recorded spread over an area of 15 to 20 acres. The settlement has come to be regarded as a classic Romano-British village, although later excavations and dating have revealed evidence of earlier habitation reaching back to the early Iron Age around 500 BC and perhaps even as far back as the Bronze or Stone Age.

The hut circles in evidence today, though not as numerous as those uncovered by the excavations of William Stanley, are remarkably well preserved and features such as entrances and internal stone furniture can be identified with ease. When in use, these stone circles formed the foundations on which wigwam-like huts with thatched roofs were erected.

Looking towards South Stack

Penrhyn Mawr

Distance: 8¼ miles

Superb walking around one of the few lowland heaths on the island. Footpaths are excellent and there are wide views to South Stack and across Caernarfon Bay to Lleyn and Snowdonia. A series of smaller headlands and coves continue the theme of the walk, followed by an inland loop through farmland.

Start: There is free parking at Penrhyn Mawr, a large open heather covered headland accessed from a short lane between Trearddur and South Stack.
Grid ref. 216 803 (Landranger 114, Explorer 262).

The walk

1. At the back of the car park there is a fingerpost indicating the coastal path both to the left and right. Take the right-hand option heading in the direction of South Stack Lighthouse. At a crossing path turn left heading southwest. At the coast bear left and follow the coastline all the way around the headland of Penrhyn Mawr. Pass round the back of Porth Ruffydd and keep following the coast bearing inland slightly at the rocky head of Dinas to go through a kissing gate. Walk round the grassy headland, passing through another gate to join a narrow path heading towards a caravan park. Join the path to Porth Dafarch beach. Cross the beach and bear right onto the signed coastal path again.

Walk around the headland and as you approach a house cross a wooden footbridge and stile and walk along an enclosed path to join the drive to a house on the right. Turn left up the drive to the road. Turn right and walk along the road for approximately 500 yards

2. Turn left down the access road to 'Isallt Fawr'. Pass houses on the left and at the end of the drive a footpath continues ahead to a ladder stile into fields. Cross the stile and walk along the right-hand field edges to an access road with houses on the right. Turn right here and walk along the access road to a T junction with a tarmac lane. Turn left along the lane and after about 100 yards take the signed field path on the right. Follow the path, which is enclosed at first, to enter a large field. Bear right through the field to a kissing gate in the far corner near bungalows. Go ahead to join an estate road and turn left.

At a T junction at the end of the road, turn left again and look for a signed footpath on the right. Turn right over the ladder stile and walk around the right-hand field edge. At a stile on the right cross over and walk ahead to a ladder stile by a gate. Cross the stile and follow the well worn footpath through an area of rocks

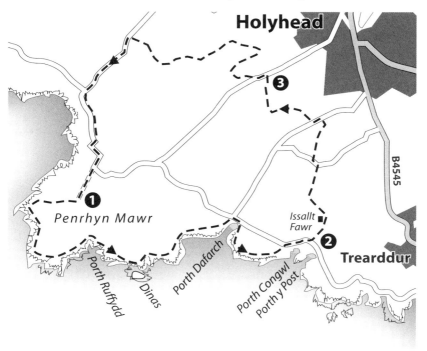

Looking north from Penrhyn Mawr to South Stack Lighthouse

and gorse. Keep to the most obvious footpath (marked by the 'St Cybi Circular Walk' symbol although many are missing at the time of writing) ignoring minor footpaths on either side. Where Holyhead Mountain comes into view with a bungalow a field or so ahead, bear right over flat rocks—initially in the direction of a distant church tower in Holyhead. Don't go into smaller fields on the right, keep ahead between gorse bushes until you reach a bungalow beyond a fence. Bear left along the fence in front of the bungalow to a gate into a lane.

3. Turn left up the lane to a stile and sign on the right. Go over the stile and walk ahead to a gap in the wall/hedge, then ahead again with Holyhead Mountain ahead to a stile in an area of gorse. Cross the stile and continue through the area of gorse and flat rocks on a visible footpath.

At a wall and kissing gate, don't go through the gate, instead turn left to a stile in the corner. Go over this stile and follow the path ahead with a wall on the right. Pass a farmhouse on the right continuing ahead. Soon the footpath bears left to pass below some small rock outcrops on the left. After the outcrops go through a kissing gate on the right and keep ahead on a good footpath with Holyhead Mountain ahead again. In the field corner bear left with the fence.

Near a farm on the right, continue ahead to a gap in the fence (waymarker) on the right. Go through the gap and keep ahead with Holyhead Mountain ahead again and a farm on the right. Soon a waymarker post directs you right to a ladder stile. Go over the stile, then bear left through a small field past a gorse covered bank on the right. Walk ahead to a gateway with an overhead power cable post beside it. Go through the gate and follow a path up the following field towards a farm. Walk ahead between the outbuildings (but to the left of the farmhouse) to a gate into a road.

Turn left along the road for about ½ mile.

Opposite a lane on the right (this is the first lane you will meet and leads to South Stack), turn left up the bank onto a new permissive footpath (signed for the coastal path) which runs parallel to the road. At the end of the path join the road for about ¼ mile before turning right down the access road to Penrhyn Mawr to complete the walk

Cymyran

Distance: 6¼ miles

Attractive walking around the tidal estuary separating Holy Island from Anglesey on a mixture of old lanes, tidal roads and the coastal path. Paths are generally good throughout.

Start: Free parking is available in the beach car park at Cymyran, 2 miles south of Caergeiliog.
Grid ref 297 755 (Landranger 114, Explorer 262).

The walk

1. Walk back along the track to join the tarmac road near the little tea shack. Continue along the road until, just before the road goes over the railway, there is an access track on the left immediately after a stone house (opposite a road on the right). Turn left here, walk down the access road and just before a large cottage (about 350 yards), turn right over a rough stone stile into a small field. In the corner of the field climb over an old iron ladder stile and turn left to a second stile. Bear right towards farm buildings to join a farm track. Turn left and walk down the track to a quiet lane which crosses the head of a marsh covered tidal creek.

2. Turn right for about 50 yards, then bear left onto a tidal road which follows the edge of mud flats to a point where another lane comes down onto the marsh. (If the tide is high it may not be possible to follow this road, but a high tide option exists along the top of the bank to the right.) Walk up the lane for almost 1 mile.

3. Close to the expressway and immediately after crossing a small river, turn left down the access road to 'Tyddyn-y-Cob'. This road runs beside a large pool on the left and as you approach an embankment containing the pool, bends sharply right to the house. Turn left here, cross the embankment to steps over the wall. Keep along the right-hand field edge crossing a wide stone wall in the corner by stone steps, then keep ahead in the following field for about 80 yards and turn right over a stone footbridge and steps. Cross a wooden walkway over boggy ground and continue straight ahead up the field to enter a quiet lane.

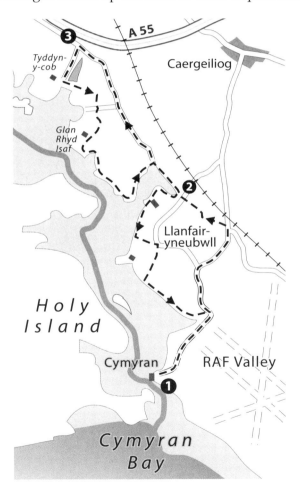

Turn left and after a few yards turn right into a lane immediately after a cottage. Pass a house on the left, and just after a gate with the sign 'Glan Rhyd Isaf' on it, bear right down to a ladder stile. Cross the field, over a double ladder stile, and then walk between two lines of telegraph poles to another ladder stile. After this turn right along a hedge to a ladder stile at 'Glan Rhyd Isaf'. The official line of the footpath carries on in front of the house and loops round in a circle to the shore, however it is recommended that you turn left down the drive straight to the shore.

From here, bear left for about 40 yards to a ladder stile on the left to join an attractive section of coastal path which overlooks the tidal estuary separating Anglesey from Holy Island. This is probably the most enjoyable section of the walk.

The shallow tidal creek which separates Holy Island from Anglesey almost dries out at low tide and a number of tidal routes crossed the sands before the modern roads were built. Prior to the building of the Stanley Embankment which now carries the A5, travellers on the Holyhead road en-route to Ireland followed a tidal route across the sands to the north of Valley. This crossing, along with the detour which could be made to Pont-rhydbont or the Four Mile Bridge, is shown on the maps of John Ogilby published in 1675. By this time ships were regularly leaving Holyhead for Ireland and this previously quiet corner of Wales would have been busy with travellers.

The beach at Cymyran

Cymyran

Keep along the field edges until you pass a small building on the right. Soon after this, bear right through a gap in the hedge / fence to join a muddy track at the mouth of a tidal creek. This is the creek visited earlier in the walk.

Turn right along the tidal road and return to the lane junction where you joined the tidal road earlier in the walk. Turn right along the lane and right again onto the signed coastal path.

In about 30 yards cross a ladder stile on the right and follow the path along the edge of fields and marsh on the right. Just before a cottage turn left away from the creek and follow the hedge on the right to a ladder stile. Cross the stile into a lane, turn right passing an access track and in about 20 yards turn right over a second stile into fields. Keep to the right-hand field edge initially, then to the right of aircraft landing lights. Eventually cross a ladder stile and bear half-left towards the little tea shack passed earlier. Cross a stile and turn right along the lane retracing outward journey.

Rhoscolyn

Distance: *2½ or 4 miles*

An enjoyable clifftop walk around Holy Island's southern tip with wide views along the west coast of the island and across Caernarfon Bay towards the mainland. Return is made by quiet lanes and field paths. Good footpaths throughout.

Start: There is a beach car park with WC facilities at Borthwen, Rhoscolyn.
Grid ref. 273 752 (Ordnance Survey Explorer 262).

The walk

1. From the car park, make your way onto the beach and turn right along the sand, or, if the tide is high, follow the path along the top of a concrete wall which backs the beach. This leads back down onto the sand and about 200 yards further on, bear right up a slipway. At the top of the rise keep right at a fork and follow the track as it bends to the right. Go along the drive to 'Bryn Eithin' and in about 20 yards, turn right through a gap in the wall on the signed path into the garden of an adjacent house. Shortly, turn left onto a well worn path between walls and gardens.

Cross the access road to 'The Point' and go through the kissing gate opposite into grazing fields. Rise through the fields now, aiming for the coastguard lookout on the skyline.

From the lookout in clear weather there is a grand view over much of Caernarfon Bay. To the north, Holyhead Mountain, with the lighthouse flashing at South Stack, can be seen in the distance, along with the chimney of the aluminium works near Holyhead. Southwards lie the sandy coves and islets around Rhoscolyn, with Rhosneigr and the headland at Aberffraw across the channel on Anglesey.

On the mainland, the peaks of Snowdonia line the horizon, from the Carneddau in the east to the Glyderau, Snowdon and the Nantlle Ridge. Further west lie the hills of the Lleyn Yr Eifl, Garn Fadryn, Mynydd Mawr, Mynydd Anlog and finally, Bardsey.

2. From the lookout, continue on the grassy path which cuts through grazing fields to Ffynnon Gwenfaen (Saint Gwenfaen's Well). This lies near the edge of the cliffs about 600 yards away. Aim just to the right of the headland which runs west from Holyhead Mountain.

This is an ancient well which captures spring water below ground level. It has stone steps, corner seats and may originally have been roofed. During the Middle Ages it was a place of pilgrimage and was believed to have the power to cure mental illness.

Beyond the well, pass through a kissing gate almost on the edge of the cliffs and follow the path along the top of a large crag overhanging the sea (take care here). The path stays close to the wall on the right which soon turns right.

It was off this headland in 1855 that the Liverpool ship, 'Southern Cross' foundered and sank after striking a submerged rock in thick fog. The ship went down rapidly giving the crew of 17 just enough time to escape in the ship's lifeboat. Incredibly, the lifeboat also struck rocks in the poor visibility and the exhausted men were forced to spend the next 12 hours on one of the many tiny rocks which can be seen breaking the surface. Their plight was noticed the following morning when the Rhoscolyn Lifeboat was sent to their aid.

Occasionally rescues ended in disaster, not just for those in trouble but also for the lifeboat crews themselves. This happened in 1920 when five Rhoscolyn volunteers including the Coxswain, Owen Owens, lost their lives in heavy seas after unsuccessfully going to the aid of the stricken steamer 'Timbo' in Caernarfon Bay.

Stay beside the wall on the right as it continues along the cliffs to the next inlet where there is a little footbridge just beyond a stile and a footpath down to the rocky cove.

At this point you have a choice. For a shorter round of about 2½ miles continue from paragraph **3a**. Alternatively, the walk can be lengthened to 4 miles by continuing along the coastal path (see paragraph **3b**.)

3a. Go through the kissing gate on the right immediately after the footbridge and cut through a small square field enclosure to pick up an old track enclosed by crumbling stone walls. Just before a large white farmhouse, turn left and follow the wall around the front of the house. In the field corner, bear half-right (arrow on post) to a kissing gate at the top of the field which leads onto the access drive. Turn left along the drive.

Just before Rhoscolyn church, turn right onto a signed footpath which follows the cemetery wall to a stone stile. Beyond this, bear half-left across a wide driveway with a large house to the right and climb over a ladder stile which leads into fields again.

Bwa Gwyn rock arch

Bear half-right through the field to a kissing gate contained by stone walls. A similar gate in the far field boundary takes you across an access track and along the field edge to a small gate by a white cottage. A short enclosed footpath leads past the cottage to the lane used to reach the beach car park at the beginning of the walk. Turn right here (straight ahead) and follow the lane back to the car park at point 1.

3b. Continue along the coastal footpath which shortly runs along the large crags which back the inlet (Porth Saint). Here the path veers half-right away from the cliff edge in the direction of the chimney of the aluminium works at Holyhead. Rejoin the coast and drop to a stile over the fence where a small inlet on the left contains a natural arch (Bwa Gwyn). Beyond this, make your way through an area of rocky outcrops to a kissing gate in the wall. This is followed shortly by a gap in the wall which leads onto a tarmac driveway to a house on the left. The path leads to a stile beside a large gate with stone pillars. Cross the stile and bear left through a rough pasture field by the wall to a metal kissing gate beside a small cove. Go through the gate and walk about 50 yards or so to the corner of the fence on your left and bear half-right towards a white house. The path soon becomes a track which leads to a T junction. Turn right and continue for about ½ mile to a second T junction.

Turn right here and follow the lane crossing a small bridge to a sharp right-hand bend by Rhoscolyn chapel. Go through a field gate immediately ahead (telephone box on left) and keep to the field edge with a small cemetery on the right. Bear left along the hedge in the top corner of the field and just before a small farmhouse, turn right through a kissing gate to cut through a small field to the road. Turn right along the lane.

At the lane signed to 'Silver Bay Holiday Park' turn left. After about 200 yards, a kissing gate on the right beside a drive leads into fields. Turn right here and follow the wall on the left through a small field to a kissing gate, then between bracken covered banks to eventually enter a larger field by a kissing gate. Cut through the centre of the field to another kissing gate and bear left along the field edge towards a cottage. Go through a kissing gate in the wall passing the cottage, then along the short access track which leads to the lane used earlier to reach the beach car park. Turn left (ahead) and follow the lane back to the car park at point 1.

Rhosneigr

Distance: *5 miles*

An easy, level walk on good lakeside footpaths with a stretch of beach walking. The route includes one of the most important prehistoric sites on the island.

Start: There is a free beach car park on the A4080 between Llanfaelog and Aberffraw.
Grid ref. 331 717 (Ordnance Survey Explorer 262).

The walk

1. Turn left out of the car park and walk along the road for about ½ mile. Ignore the first footpath sign on the left by 'Penlon Cottage' instead, continue to the second signed path where a large ladder stile leads over the wall. Walk ahead along the field edge with overgrown walls on the left. At the end of the walls the right of way continues ahead across a large field to enter a track by a ladder stile with a bungalow on the right. Turn right along the track to the road.

Turn right over the bridge then cross the road and turn left down an unmade access road. Pass several houses on the right and immediately before the gateway to the last house, bear left onto a footpath which follows the edge of Llyn Maelog. At the head of the lake cross a small footbridge and keep left around the shore edge.

Llyn Maelog was originally an inlet from the sea which has been dammed and turned into a fresh water pool by the sand dunes of Tywyn Llyn. Its formation is similar to that of Llyn Coron near Aberffraw which has also been isolated from the sea by wind blown sand forming the massive dunes of Tywyn Aberffraw. The lake is fairly shallow for its size being rarely more than seven feet deep and is often used for canoeing and windsurfing.

The reed fringed shore gives excellent cover for a number of birds and nesting species which include great crested grebe, little grebe, coot, tufted duck, moorhen and mallard.

The final section of footpath is along a new all user board walk.

2. At the road cross diagonally leftwards and walk down the road opposite. Where this forks bear left and at a second fork keep left again. This sandy track eventually leads through the dunes onto the beach (Traeth Llydan). Turn left along the beach.

Looking across Llyn Maelog to Rhosneigr

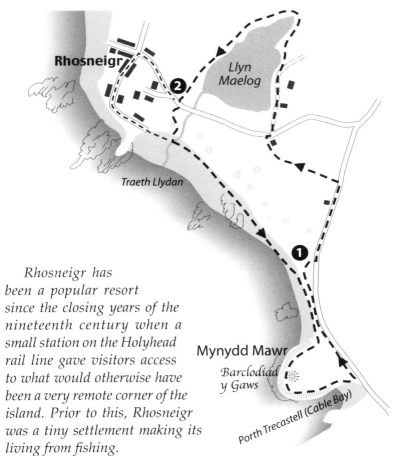

Rhosneigr has been a popular resort since the closing years of the nineteenth century when a small station on the Holyhead rail line gave visitors access to what would otherwise have been a very remote corner of the island. Prior to this, Rhosneigr was a tiny settlement making its living from fishing.

The name Rhosneigr is thought to be derived from 'Yneigr' 'a maiden' and 'rhos' meaning 'moor'—its English translation would thus be 'Moor of the Maid'. The word 'Rhos' appears in many Welsh place names and moors are still a familiar part of the Welsh landscape. In Rhosneigr's case the 'moor' referred to is undoubtedly the large area of dunes to the north of the village known as Tywyn Trewan. In earlier centuries this area would have been a wilderness of marsh, lakes and tidal sands inundated by the sea. Centuries of dune formation have provided a defence from the sea and *created an ideal location for the RAF airbase which now occupies the western half of the common.*

(For Rhosneigr village where there are shops, pubs and cafés, turn right along the road. In the centre of the village there is a post office and convenience store on the crossroads. Turn left along High Street where there are shops and cafés. This eventually curves left and becomes 'Lôn Traeth Llydan', with houses on the left, then on both sides. At a distinct left turn take the beach access road straight ahead which takes you down onto Traeth Llydan, signed for the coastal path.)

Walk along two large stretches of sand and one smaller cove separated by low rocks before joining the coastal footpath which skirts the headland of Mynydd Mawr.

At the end of the headland is one of the most famous prehistoric relics on the island — Baclodiad y Grawes. A fine burial chamber from the Neolithic period and in one of the most magnificent settings, it was 'restored' following excavation in the 1950s. A modern entrance and iron gate allow the visitor access to the inner chamber which is covered by a large concrete roof quite out of character with the ancient stones of the original mound. This restoration work has however, protected one of the most important features of the chamber — a number of stones decorated with spirals, zig-zags and lozenges. This feature links it with similar Irish tombs found today in the Boyne Valley. The name translates into 'Giantess's Apronfull' and referred to the large number of stones which were undoubtedly part of the original mound.

Continue round into Porth Trecastell (Cable Bay). Walk through the beach car park and turn left along the road. After about 300-400 yards, look for the coastal footpath sign on the left near a small parking area. Just before the beach the path forks—keep right by a small white cottage and follow the path along the top of the dunes back to the car park.

Aberffraw

Distance: *4½ miles*

An easy, almost level walk along an attractive section of the coast with wide views across Caernarfon Bay to the hills of the Lleyn Peninsula. Excellent footpaths throughout.

Start: There is free parking available for a number of cars on common land beside the old bridge at Aberffraw. *Grid ref. 356 689 (Ordnance Survey Explorer 262).*

The walk

1. Cross the old bridge and turn left immediately onto an unmade tidal road which runs beside the river. Where the road bears left onto the sand, continue along the shore to the mouth of the river.

(If the water is high or the shore too wet, turn right onto the signed coastal path, then turn left between gardens. This path takes you back to the shore where a low wall runs above the sand. Follow the path along the top of the wall, then drop onto the sand just before a cottage and continue to the river mouth.)

Originally, Aberffraw was open to the sea and even enjoyed a brief period of prosperity as a small port. Over the centuries however, the estuary on which it lies has become filled with wind-blown sand with the result that today over half a mile of sand dunes separate it from the sea. In its original state, the estuary would have been something like the nearby Malltraeth Sands and extended inland for over two miles. Llyn Coron, near Bodorgan Station, which is now a fresh water lake, marks the original limit of the estuary.

Today, you will find nothing at Aberffraw to suggest its past

Aberffraw has one of the most stunning beaches in Wales

importance as the administrative centre for the kings and princes, not just of Anglesey, but the whole of North Wales. For eight hundred years, Welsh kings and princes used the royal palace at Aberffraw as a base in their fight against invasions from Irish, Saxons, Vikings and finally Normans.

The palace was established by Cunedda, who came from Strathclyde with his sons and a large army of fighting men, to rid North Wales of Irish tribes who had attacked and overrun the kingdom, following the Roman withdrawal. Cunedda was a powerful Celtic chieftain who was able to pass on to his sons a vast kingdom which encompassed much of present day North Wales. His grandson, Cadwallon, who inherited the northern kingdom which would become Gwynedd, is credited with finally ridding Wales of the Irish in a last battle on Anglesey about AD 470. Other rulers associated with Aberffraw include Cadwallon's son, Maelgwyn Gwynedd, who granted land for the founding of monasteries at Holyhead and Penmon in the mid sixth century and Rhodri Mawr (Rhodri the Great 844-878), who ruled much of Wales from his seat at Aberffraw, as did Llywelyn Fawr (the Great). Other prominent names include Gruffydd ap Cynan who died in 1137 at the remarkable age of 82, his son Owain Gwynedd and Llywelyn 'the Last', whose defeat by Edward I in 1282 brought Welsh independence to an end.

With such a long period of use—something like the period which separates our own time from that of Edward I—it is perhaps surprising that no trace of the palace is now to be seen. The reason for this is that throughout its long history it was built entirely from wood, a fact which made possible its partial destruction by the Vikings in 968. The

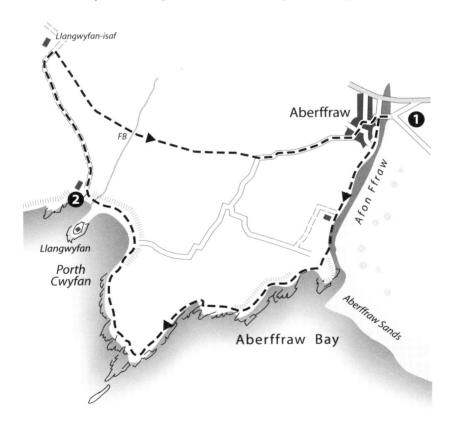

building of castles and churches from stone did not really begin until after the Norman conquest and even then, the earliest motte and bailey castles were usually of timber construction. Although this may seem strange as we look at the bare, treeless landscape of today, for much of the period that the palace was in use, Anglesey was thickly wooded. By the fourteenth century however, timber was evidently in shorter supply—in 1317 the palace was demolished and its timbers used to repair Caernarfon Castle.

Near the mouth of the river, bear right through a kissing gate onto the coastal footpath. Before you do this, it is worth heading left across the grassy headland for a fine view of the bay.

This is one of the most beautiful bays in Wales and is perhaps seen at its best on a clear summer evening when the crowds have left. Across the shallow clear waters of Caernarfon Bay, the blue outlines of Gryn Ddu, Yr Eifl and the hills of the Lleyn Peninsula line the horizon, while the higher peaks of Snowdonia peep over the headland at the end of the bay.

The coastal path from here is easy to follow and keeps to the edge of the low rocks with occasional departures into small coves and onto wave-cut rocks. Keep your eyes open for grey seals which can frequently be seen in these shallow waters. Continue to Porth Cwyfan, a wide bay with a tiny church on a small island. A short walk along the shingle beach takes you onto the island which is cut off at high tide.

This tiny isolated church dedicated to Saint Cwyfan, was founded in the seventh century and rebuilt in stone during the twelfth century. In the centuries that followed, it was added to a number of times before being fully restored in the nineteenth century. Despite this, it has managed to retain its original simple form. The stone wall which surrounds the island was built during the nineteenth century restoration to counteract severe erosion problems. Outside the church a few scattered gravestones remain from the eighteenth century, along with a memorial to Frank Morley, a youngster of 20 who drowned in nearby Porth Trecastell.

2. Continue along the beach past the church. At the far end of the bay an access track reaches down onto the beach beside a small cottage (don't confuse this with a lane passed earlier *before* the church). Walk up the track passing the Anglesey Racing Circuit on your left (mainly out of sight but not out of earshot).

Look for a signed footpath on your right just before a large house (Llangwyfan-isaf) on the left. Go through the kissing gate and walk ahead through the centre of a large open field to cross a stile. Continue ahead in the following field to a kissing gate and footbridge over a stream. Cross the footbridge and follow the right of way ahead along the left-hand field edge to cross a farm track almost in the top corner of the field. Go through a kissing gate here and bear half-left through the field to a footbridge over a ditch. Head half-left again across the following field to steps near an old kissing gate. Go ahead along the field edge to a lane.

Turn left along the lane and walk back to Aberffraw. In the centre of the village by the post office, turn right. Pass 'Y Goron' ('The Crown') pub and continue down to cross the old bridge to complete the walk.

The tiny church of Saint Cwyfan

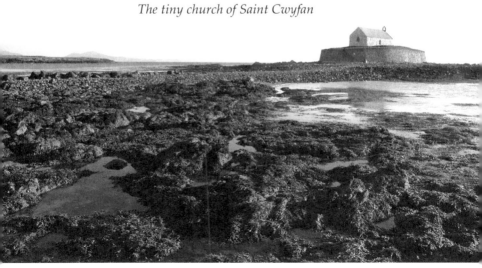

Ynys Llanddwyn

Distance: *8¾ miles*

An exploration of forest tracks, an island once the goal of the love sick, and one of the largest and most spectacular beaches in Wales. Footpaths and forest tracks are excellent throughout.

Start: There is a small forest car park at the northern edge of the Newborough Forest about 1 mile south of the village of Malltraeth on the A4080.
Grid ref. 412 671. (Ordnance Survey Explorer 263).

The walk

1. From the car park turn right onto a path which runs parallel to the road (back towards Newborough) and is signed with the coastal footpath logo. In about 250 yards, and opposite the entrance to 'Llyn Parc Mawr' forest car park and picnic area, turn right onto a broad forest road. Follow the road for about ½ mile.

At post number 33 (first major forest road on the left) turn left onto another good forest road. Ignore any minor tracks/paths before this. Pass a small ruined cottage on the left and follow the forest road as it rises and eventually curves right. About 400 yards further on take the first obvious broad path on the left which runs at right angles to the forest road.

This path is very straight and eventually brings you to the edge of the woods with fields ahead. Turn right with the path and where this forks in 100 yards or so, keep right on a less obvious path.

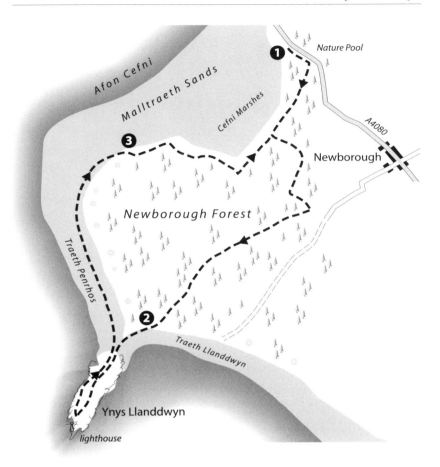

The Newborough Forest was planted in the 1950s to stabilise a vast area of moving sand dunes formed over the last 700 years by prevailing southwesterly winds. Today, it is a working forest producing over 10,000 tons of timber per year and has been designated as a Site of Special Scientific Interest.

The trees, mainly Corsican Pine, thrive in the sandy soil and are not harmed by the salt spray thrown up during winter storms. They have stabilised the dunes which have suffered frequent erosion problems over *the centuries. As early as Elizabethan times, attempts to stabilise the dunes by planting marram grass were made after over-grazing damaged the thin soil cover. This led to vast areas of valuable agricultural land, which had been farmed since the Middle Ages, being buried by several metres of wind-blown sand.*

The introduction of marram grass gave rise to a thriving cottage industry making ropes, baskets and mats which lasted until the end of the last century. Today the lime rich soil (from tiny shell fragments) of the older inland dunes, produces a colourful display of wild flowers in the summer months.

This sensitive area is now protected and managed and walkers are reminded to keep to the designated rights of way to avoid further erosion.

Keep ahead at an obvious crossing track (post 25) and in a further ¾ mile a forest road joins from the right. Keep straight ahead here and make your way to a small parking area almost on the edge of the forest. Take the obvious track down to the beach and turn right along the sand to Ynys Llanddwyn.

2. A short walk across the sand which separates it from the mainland takes you onto the island. Aim for a large information board and follow the track immediately behind the board down to the Pilots' Cottages near the lighthouse.

Overlooking the bay at the southern tip of the island are a number of relics from the island's maritime past. The row of tiny cottages to the right of the path once housed the Llanddwyn Pilots and their families. These individuals took turns to man the lighthouse, built in 1845 and now abandoned, and guide shipping into nearby Caernarfon harbour. They also acted as lifeboat men and carried out a number of daring rescues during the nineteenth century. The small canon which stands in front of the cottages was used throughout this period to summon the lifeboat and crew in times of distress. The Pilots' Cottages were renovated in 1977 by Anglesey Borough Council and two are regularly open to the public where an exhibition and a series of period rooms can be viewed.

The remains of 'The Greek Ship' *on Traeth Penrhos*

The smaller white tower down to the left was originally a navigation beacon built in 1819. In 1972, this structure was found to be more suitable for the modern automatic beacon than the lighthouse which is now disused.

Part of the exhibition tells the story of Saint Dwynwen, who is said to have lived here in the fifth century and gave the island its name. In her younger days, Dwynwen fell in love with a prince by the name of Maelon, who was so infatuated by the young maiden that he could not wait for marriage and tried to seduce her. The resistance she made resulted in Maelon's rejection.

The story says that while she mourned her loss, an angel visited her and gave her a healing potion, which cured her of her love and turned Maelon into ice. Dwynwen then vowed to become a nun.

The shrine which she established here attracted pilgrims in great numbers in the years that followed, particularly from the love sick. She is said to have used the magical powers of a secret well to determine whether or not a loved one was faithful.

This story is a fine example of how the superstitions and beliefs of the old Celtic religion quickly found their way into the early Christian church. References to healing potions, magic wells and wicked princes being turned into ice, echo the stories of the Mabinogion, *a series of folklore stories which predate Christianity by several centuries.*

Today, spectacular scenery and miles of secluded beach are the main attraction for the visitor. To the south, the serrated outlines of Snowdonia, followed by the blue silhouettes of Yr Eifl (The Rivals) and the smaller hills of Lleyn form an impressive backdrop to the wide sweep of Caernarfon Bay and the golden sands of Traeth Llanddwyn.

From the old lighthouse, a good footpath leads along the northern edge of the island passing the ruins of Eglwyseg Dwynwen on the right.

These are the ruins of a sixteenth century church dedicated to Saint Dwynwen, said to be built on the site of her original church established over 1,100 years earlier. The arched windows are edged with sandstone blocks and the outline of a small churchyard can be traced in the grass outside the building. The present ruinous state of the church is said have been due in part to the removal of timbers for boat building and stone for the navigation beacon at the beginning of the nineteenth century.

Leave the island and turn left along Traeth Penrhos, one of the grandest and most isolated beaches in Anglesey. Follow the sand for about 1½ miles, before the dunes become lower and curve northeast into the vast expanse of Malltraeth Sands, the tidal estuary of Afon Cefni.

Part way along the beach, the remains of a wreck can often be seen breaking the waves at low tide. This is known locally as Y llong Groeg, meaning 'The Greek Ship'. She was the brig' Athena', which foundered in December 1852 en-route to Liverpool. Fourteen crew were saved from the wreck by the Llanddwyn lifeboat.

This vast stretch of tidal sands was the inspiration for much of the work of the late wildlife illustrator Charles Tunnicliffe. He was born in 1901 in eastern Cheshire and moved to Malltraeth with his wife in 1947. His house 'Shorelands', looked out over the estuary and provided the naturalist with enough material to last him a dozen lifetimes. He died at Malltraeth in 1979.

Large as the estuary is today, originally it reached over 12 miles inland almost to the outskirts of Llangefni. Like Traeth Mawr near Porthmadog, reclamation schemes at the beginning of the nineteenth century turned much of the estuary into farmland. This was accomplished by means of a seawall or 'cob', which spans the sands near Malltraeth.

The estuary is of national importance to the numerous species of wildfowl which stop to feed here on their long migratory flights between Arctic Norway and Africa.

3. Just before the sand dunes end, bear right onto a path through the dunes to join a sandy track which runs along the edge of the forest. Turn left along the track and continue, with the trees on your right and the salt marshes on your left, for about 1 mile.

A few hundred yards after entering the woods proper, turn left at an obvious T junction. Follow the broad forestry road back to the road (A4080) and turn left back to the car park.

The nearby village of Newborough came into existence in 1303, to accommodate the villagers evicted from Llanfaes when Edward I began the building of his new garrison town at Beaumaris. The move created a 'new borough' from which the village gets its name. However, the exposed location soon created problems for the villagers. Over-grazing and the removal of trees on the nearby dunes of Newborough Warren soon damaged the delicate soil cover and by the time of Elizabeth I, wind-blown sand had buried much of the village's valuable agricultural land.

In an attempt to stabilise the dunes, marram grass was introduced which, in the nineteenth century, gave rise to the flourishing basket and rope making industry already mentioned.

Newborough Warren & Abermenai

Distance: *3½ or 6¾ miles*

This walk explores the extreme southern tip of the island—a wild expanse of wind-blown dunes, tidal sands and marshes. If you intend to complete the longer option to Abermenai Point, time the walk to coincide with a low or falling tide enabling you to cross the estuary safely. If you can not do this, the shorter walk can be completed safely at any state of the tide.

Start: Take the A4080 from Dwyran to Newborough. At Pen-lôn there is a small roundabout where a right turn continues to Newborough. Take the lane straight ahead which leads to a small car park by Llyn Rhos-Ddu.
Grid ref. 426 647 (Landranger 114, Explorer 263).

The walk

1. Turn left out of the car park and take the signed coastal path with the reeds of Llyn Rhos-Ddu to the right. After about 700 yards there is a small kissing gate on the left along with an information board and a grass farm track on the right. Turn left through the kissing gate and walk through the dunes of Newborough Warren National Nature Reserve for about 1½ miles. It is important that walkers keep to the right of way which is marked at frequent intervals by white posts.

Newborough Warren has been a sensitive and problematic area since Elizabethan times when over grazing resulted in the loss of valuable agricultural land beneath several metres of wind-blown sand. Today it provides a haven for wildlife being one of the largest sand dune systems in Britain. It is also designated as a national nature reserve in recognition of its rich flora and fauna.

Summer is the best time to visit the dunes when they are carpeted with wild flowers. Orchids are particularly notable and are often found growing in profusion. From June common spotted, pyramidal and marsh orchids are in flower. In July the dune hollows are full of marsh helleborines and the rarer dune helleborine can also be found. As the summer progresses and the orchids wither, delicate white wintergreen and grass of parnassus take their place and later purple flowered autumn gentian. The rich supply of nectar from the varied flowers attracts a wealth of insects including the distinctive red and black day-flying burnet moth.

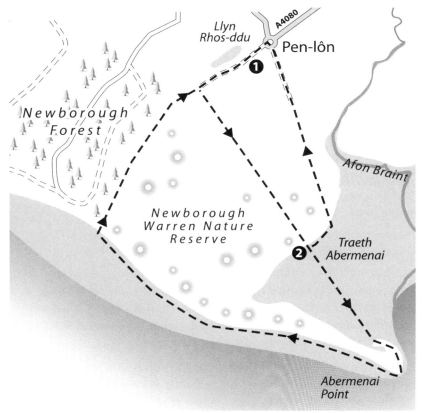

Newborough Warren — the path through the dunes

Also, look for cormorants and other sea birds. Ynys yr Adar ('Bird Island') near Ynys Llanddwyn supports over one per cent of the British breeding population of the Cormorant.

The area is equally special in winter when the mud flats and salt marshes are important wintering grounds for wildfowl and waders.

The path comes to an abrupt halt on the edge of the vast tidal sands of Traeth Abermenai.

Over on the mainland you will see the town of Caernarfon with its famous castle built by Edward I after his conquest of Wales in the thirteenth century. Behind the town, the skyline is filled with a panorama of Snowdonia's highest peaks, while to the west, the pointed tops of Yr Eifl peep over the dunes at Abermenai Point.

2. (Longer walk) If the water is low or falling you will have time to cross the estuary to Abermenai Point. Take a direct line aiming for the left-hand end of the distant line of sand dunes (about

1 mile). Do not ignore the warning given at the beginning of this chapter regarding suitable times for crossing the sands to Abermenai Point.

Prior to the bridging of the Menai Strait by Thomas Telford in 1826, a number of ferries crossed to the mainland from Abermenai Point. The ferry which served this southern end of the Strait gave the islanders access to the market at Caernarfon. The dangerous nature of the crossing is illustrated by the fact that several ferry boats came to grief with many fatalities.

Perhaps the most tragic was that which occurred on 5 December 1785. The ferry left Caernarfon with 55 passengers on board about one hour before low tide. Halfway across, the boat hit a sand bank, tipped over and could not be re-floated. When the tide turned she began taking in water leaving the passengers stranded on the shrinking sand bar in the middle of the channel until one by one they were swept away to perish in the freezing water. Only one person survived, a man named Hugh Williams from Aberffraw who spent an over two hours in the water.

From Abermenai Point walk northwest along the beach towards Ynys Llanddwyn, a route which lies outside the restricted area of the nature reserve (2¾ miles). At the edge of the conifers of the Newborough Forest (before you reach Ynys Llanddwyn), turn right onto the signed coastal path which will take you back to the car park to complete the route.

2. (Shorter walk) If you have any doubts about crossing the sands to Abermenai, or prefer a shorter walk, turn left and follow the path along the edge of the estuary for about 500 yards and look for a post which marks the right of way back to Pen-lôn. Turn left here and follow the path across the dunes again to join a lane by houses and a picnic area. Continue straight ahead along the lane and at the roundabout turn left to complete the walk.

The unusual sculptures in the car park depict bundles of marram grass which were gathered locally for a thriving basket making industry carried out in the nineteenth century.

Mara Books

Mara Books publish a range of walking books for Cheshire and North Wales and have the following list to date. A complete list of current titles is available on our web site:

www.marabooks.co.uk *or*
www.northerneyebooks.com

North Wales

Walking on the Lleyn Peninsula

ISBN 978-1-902512-15-0. A collection of circular walks exploring the wild and beautiful coastline and hills of the Lleyn Peninsula.

Circular Walks in the Conwy Valley

ISBN 978-1-902512-11-2. A collection of circular walks which explore the varied scenery of this beautiful valley from the Great Orme to Betws-y-Coed.

Walking in Snowdonia *Volume 1*

ISBN 978-1-902512-06-8. A series of circular walks exploring the beautiful and dramatic valleys in the northern half of the Snowdonia National Park.

A pocket guide to Snowdon

ISBN 978-1-902512-16-7. A guide to all the recognised routes of ascent, from the six 'Classic Paths' to the many lesser known and less frequented routes. Includes a full colour relief map.

A pocket guide to Snowdonia's best Mountain Walks

ISBN 978-1-902512-19-8. A guide to the best walks and scrambles to be enjoyed in the mountains of the Snowdownia National Park.